Contents　目錄

编者的话

这不是一本词典，但却有部分词典的功能；这不是一本成语故事书，但却有不少成语，还注明了出处；这不是一本中英翻译的名人名言，这本名言语录，却有中英对照的效果。这本书通俗而不庸俗，轻松而不轻佻，幽默而不肉麻，认真而不呆板。通过这本书，外国人可以较容易地了解一些中国文化；中国人可以多学习一些外国的格言；家长和孩子沟通时，可以多一些益智的内容；教师们可以多一些参考的资料；在社交场合上，可以多一些博古通今的话题。这本书，能令你边读边发出会心的微笑，一书在手，其乐无穷。这本充满哲理的书，适合你我，适合每一个人。

"哲学"往往会给人误解为：其一，哲学无非是说一些似是而非、模棱两可的道理；其二，哲学只是在玩弄一些枯燥乏味、艰涩难明的文字。编完了这本书，我对哲学有了更新的体验。读了这本书，相信你对哲学亦会有完全崭新的认识。

"罗马不是一天建成的。"；"己所不欲，勿施于人。"；"冬天来了，春天还会远吗？"；"但愿人长久，千里共婵娟"……古今中外的先哲前贤，留下了许许多多这样的佳句给我们。有励志的，有歌颂爱情的，有唤醒一个人的良知的、有在困境中注入希望的……这些句子，文字精练、简洁有力、一语中的、意味深长，充满了幽默与睿智。有些我们天天挂在嘴边，却不知道原来是谁讲的；有些我们耳熟能详，也很想知道它们的出处。

"千里之行，始于足下。"正是老子两千多年前的这句名言，触发了我们的灵感，有了这个大胆的构思，设计了这片园地，把几百句精彩的金句，巧妙地配对起来。仿如古今中外的国家元首、著名学者、成功商人……在历史的长河中纵横进退，划破地域国界、穿越时空，或闲谈，或切磋，交换彼此的真知灼见，享受那一刻相见恨晚的心灵沟通。我们在读这本书的时候，也好像参与了其中，同时漫步在这文化之旅上。

通过这样的安排，我们对哲学不再感到高深莫测了，不再感到苍白沉闷了，不再抗拒了。相反的，只感到它亲切、熟悉、有道理、趣味盎然了。

正如庄子所说："其作始也简，其作毕也必巨。"编撰这本书，我们参阅了大量的书籍，投入了大量的精神和时间，不断添加上新的句子，筛选掉不适当的句子，尽量找到正确的出处。求证再求证、校对再校对，务求精益求精，

可以说达到日以继夜、废寝忘食的地步。在得到不少前辈好友的支持、
鼓励和帮助下，这本书终于完成了。回想这两年来，绝大部分搜集名句、
配对和校对的工作，都只有我们两人去做。每一天，用一滴一滴的汗水，
合作无间地培育出此株奇花异卉。看着她萌芽，看着她长大，
看着她出落得超凡脱俗，越看越觉得她美丽。希望读者们，
有一种惊艳的感觉，能闻到她的芳香，越看越喜欢。
由于水平有限，书中相信仍有不少错误的地方。还望各位读者、
各位前辈不吝赐教、指正，先此谢谢大家。

李邱湄

ConfuciusMeetsShakespeare@gmail.com
www.ConfuciusMeetsShakespeare.tumblr.com

Preface

Have you ever hungered for a dish that was nowhere served, or longed to play a game that was nowhere sold? <u>Confucius Meets Shakespeare</u> is a book I have always wanted to read but could never find. Tired of waiting, I started on what you now hold in hand. Let me tell you about this book I never found.

I wanted to find a book that matched the greatest wit of the western world with that of the east—each in its own tongue, preserving in full its own force; a book that puts side by side a poet from one world next to a poet from another, speaking the same thoughts and using their own words; to see Confucius juxtaposed against Shakespeare only to find their ideas overlapping rather than clashing; to find that great minds do proverbially think alike—across time and space. I have several reasons why I wanted to read a book like this.

First, this book provides practical help for all who feel caught in between the Chinese-English cultural vortex: immigrant parents who struggle to communicate cultural values with their children, translators who are faced with cultural impasses, students on a deadline scrounging for a pithy quote, and any speaker looking for rhetorical inspiration in an international setting.

The second reason is that it will help bridge, what may appear at first to be an impassable chasm, the cultural misunderstanding between the East and the West. Confucius Meets Shakespeare will allow one culture to understand another through the thinkers of one's own and to feel the sorrow of another through the poets of one's own. I am convinced that the deeper things are universal. Language may be conventional, but truth is not; people may shout with different voices, but the pain or pleasure behind it has always been the same—for love, for glory, for pain, and for loss.

The third reason is less praiseworthy; I am simply tired of seeing the depth of Chinese verses reduced to colloquial advice. The translations are technically accurate and the comparisons are somewhat intelligible but, like TV dinners, the product is barely palatable, often upsetting, and never as delightful as the original. The fault is not in the translator; attempting to literally transpose a culture word for word is as futile as trying to sing the color green. The task is, for all intents and purposes, impossible. This nagging dissatisfaction I experienced in reading other bilingual quote books coupled with my conviction that wisdom is universal led me to ask, "why bother translating at all?" If the purpose of translation is to gather meaning from the words of a foreign thinker, and if someone equally respectable from one's own culture has already expressed the meaning, why risk losing the punch of practiced wit, the subtle rhythm in the flow of words, to translate what is essentially already understood? Why not just put side by side the two quotes, which essentially say the same thing?

Those questions were ultimately answered when I met Amy Lee, a Chinese instructor who happened to share my same passion (or frustration), and the two of us decided to compile Confucius Meets Shakespeare. Being fully aware of the possibility of misquotation, if you, our gracious reader, happen to find any, we would be very grateful if you would send us an e-mail telling us of the mistake. I thank you in advance for your time and I hope you will enjoy reading these quotes as much as we had in matching them.

Truly Yours,

Joseph Tsang
ConfuciusMeetsShakespeare@gmail.com
www.ConfuciusMeetsShakespeare.tumblr.com

Chapter 1

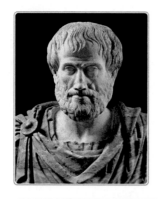

Without friends no one would choose to live, though he had all other goods.

——Aristotle
(Ancient Greece Philosopher)
亚里士多德（古希腊哲学家）

没有友谊的人生，
是枯燥的人生。

——李俊琪（国画家）
Li Junqi (Artist)

You cannot be friends upon any other terms than upon the terms of equality.

——Woodrow Wilson
(28th President of the United States)
威尔逊（美国第二十八任总统）

志同道合。

——西晋·陈寿（史学家）
《三国志· 魏志·陈思 王植传》
Chen Shou (Historian)

道不同，不相为谋。

——春秋·鲁·孔子（思想家、教育家）
Confucius (Philosopher & Educator)

On Friendship 友谊

My father always used to say that when you die, if you've got five real friends, you've had a great life.

——Lido Anthony Lee Iacocca
(American Businessman, Former CEO of Chrysler)
李•艾科卡(美国商人、克莱斯勒公司前首席执行官)

人生得一知己足矣。

——鲁迅(文学家、思想家、革命家)
《鲁迅全集》赠瞿秋白之辞
Lu Xun (Writer, Philosopher & Revolutionist)

一个人生活，可以很快乐。 可是，只有一个人， 便不能说是幸福。

——张小娴(言情小说家)
Zhang Xiaoxian (Novelist)

No man can be happy without a friend, nor be sure of his friend till he is unhappy.

——Thomas Fuller
(English Churchman & Historian)
富勒(英国牧师、史学家)

There is no hope of joy except in human relations.

——Antoine de Sainte-Exupéry
(French Writer & Aviator)
安东尼•埃克苏佩里(法国作家、空军飞行员)

古今中外隽语妙对

You can make more friends in two months by becoming more interested in other people than you can in two years by trying to get people interested in you.

——Dale Carnegie
(American Self-improvement Writer)
戴尔·卡耐基(美国自我完善作家)

一个永远也不欣赏别人的人，也就是一个永远也不被别人欣赏的人。

——汪国真(诗人)
Wang Guozhen (Poet)

近朱者赤，近墨者黑。

——西晋•傅玄(政治家、文学家、思想家)
《太子少傅箴》
Fu Xuan (Politician, Writer & Philosopher)

Association begets assimilation.

——Thomas Watson Jr.
(Former IBM Chairman)
托马斯·沃森(前IBM董事长)

Tell me thy company, and I'll tell thee what thou art.

——Miguel de Cervantes
(Spanish Novelist & Poet)
塞万提斯(西班牙小说家、诗人)

 On Friendship 友谊

Be slow to fall into friendship; but when thou art in, continue firm and constant.

——Socrates
(Ancient Greek Philosopher)
苏格拉底(古希腊哲学家)

先淡后浓，先疏后密，
先远后近，交友之道也。

——胡适(学者、诗人、哲学家)
《胡氏家训》
Hu Shi (Scholar, Poet & Philosopher)

友谊是易碎品。从来就没有
"坚如盘石"的友谊。倘能坚如
盘石，那已不是友谊，必是仇恨了。

——鲍吉尔·原野(散文家)
Yuan Ye (Essaiest)

Friendship is always a sweet responsibility, never an opportunity.

——Kahlil Gibran
(Lebanese-American Poet, Painter, Sculptor & Philosopher)
凯希勒·纪伯伦(黎巴嫩裔美国诗人、画家、雕塑家、哲学家)

Friendships are fragile things, and require as much handling as any other fragile and precious thing.

——Randolph Silliman Bourne
(American Progressive Writer)
伦道夫·西利曼·伯恩(美国进步作家)

4

古今中外隽语妙对

> In adversity we know our friends.

——Vladimir Ilich Lenin
(Founder of Russian Soviet Socialist Republic)
列宁(苏维埃社会主义共和国创始人)

> 患难见真情。

——明·东鲁古狂生
《醉醒石》

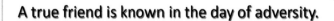

> 疾风知劲草，板荡识诚臣。

——唐·李世民
(太宗皇帝、政治家、军事家)
《赠萧瑀》
Li Shimin (Emperor, Politician & Militarist)

> A true friend is known in the day of adversity.

——Marcus Tullius Cicero
(Ancient Roman Orator, Politician & Philosopher)
西塞罗(古罗马政治家、哲学家)

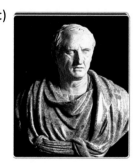

> The firmest friendships have been formed in mutual adversity, as iron is most strongly united by the fiercest flame.

——Charles Caleb Colton
(English Writer & Collector)
科尔顿(英国作家、收藏家)

On Friendship 友谊

A friend in need is a friend indeed.

——Quintus Ennius
(Founder of Roman Poetry)
昆图斯·恩纽斯(罗马诗创始人)

雪中送炭。

——明·凌蒙初(小说家)
《初刻拍案惊奇》
Ling Mengchu (Novelist)

Purchase not friends by gifts; when thou
ceases to give, such will cease to love.

——Thomas Fuller
(English Churchman & Historian)
富勒(英国牧师、史学家)

君子之交淡如水，
小人之交甘若醴。

——战国·宋·庄子(思想家、哲学家、文学家)
《庄子·山木》
Zhuangzi (Philosopher & Writer)

以财交者，财尽而交绝。

——《战国策·楚策一》

6

All the splendor in the world is not worth a good friend.

——Voltaire
(French Philosopher, Historian & Writer)
伏尔泰（法国哲学家、史学家、作家）

万两黄金容易得，
知心一个也难求。

——清·曹雪芹（小说家）
《红楼梦》
Cao Xueqin (Novelist)

人生贵相知，何必金与钱。

——唐·李白（浪漫主义诗人）
《赠友人三首》之二
Li Bai (Poet)

千金易得，知己难求。

——中国谚语
Chinese Proverb

On Friendship 友谊

The very best have had their calumniators and the every worst their panegyrists.

——Charles Caleb Colton
(English Writer & Collector)
科尔顿（英国作家、收藏家）

曹操也有知心友，关公亦有对头人。

——谚语
Chinese Proveb

No friend comes to visit you once you lose your fortune.

——Ovidius
(Roman Poet)
奥维德（古罗马诗人）

有钱有酒多兄弟，急难何曾见一人。

——《增广贤文》
Chinese Proverb

贫居闹市无人问， 富在深山有远亲。

——《增广贤文》
Chinese Proverb

古今中外隽语妙对

Chapter 2

When we lose one we love, our bitterest tears are called for by the memory of hours when we loved not enough.

——Maurice Maeterlinck
(Belgian Poet & Playwright)
莫里斯·梅特科林(比利时诗人、剧作家)

此情可待成追忆，
只是当时已惘然。

——唐·李商隐(诗人)
《锦瑟》
Li Shangyin (Poet)

One hour of right-down love is worth an age of dully living on.

——Aphra Behn
(British Playwright)
阿弗拉·班恩(英国剧作家)

不在乎天长地久，
只在乎曾经拥有。

——朱家鼎(广告创作人)
Zhu Jiading

Love & Marriage　　愛情&婚姻

How many merits one sees in those one likes! How many faults in those one dislikes! Yet people fancy they see with their eyes.

——Augustus William Hare & Julius Charles Hare (British Theologian)

奥古斯塔斯·威廉·黑尔和朱利叶斯·查尔斯·黑尔（英国神学家）

人一旦发现爱情，所有的缺点就变成可解释的和可改变的，甚至索性就成了优点。

——柏杨（学者、作家）
Bai Yang (Scholar & Author)

To love, you lose your heart, only to find you have gained it back.

——Victor Marie Hugo (French Playwright & Novelist)

雨果（法国剧作家、小说家）

爱情使一个人抛舍了自己的一半给爱人，又从爱人那里得到了新的一半。

——陈超南
Chen Chaonan

> Sex without love is a meaningless experience, but as far as meaningless experiences go, it's pretty damn good.
>
> ——Woody Allen
> (American Comedian & Director)
> 伍迪·艾伦（美国喜剧演员、导演）

> 没有爱情的性欲与
> 没有性欲的爱情同样荒谬。
>
> ——张乐天（教授）
> Zhang Letian (Professor)

> There is hardly any activity, any enterprise, which is started with such tremendous hopes and expectations, and yet which fails so regularly, as love.
>
> ——Erich Fromm
> (American Psychologist)
> 弗洛姆（美国心理学家）

> 爱是人性中最活泼、最美丽、
> 最有生命力的因素，也是最矛盾、
> 最痛苦、最不稳定的因素。
>
> ——关鸿（记者）
> Guan Hong (Reporter)

Love & Marriage　　愛情&婚姻

诗人常说爱情是盲目的，但
不盲目的爱毕竟更健全更可靠。

——傅雷（翻译家、作家、文学评论家）
《傅雷家书》
Fu Lei (Translator, Author & Critic)

Love is not blind—it sees more, not less.
But because it sees more, it is willing to see less.

——Julius Gordon
(Judean Orator & Rabbi)
朱利叶斯·戈登（犹太演说家、教师）

"Love is said to be blind, but I know some
fellows who can see twice as much in their
sweethearts as I can."

——Josh Billings
(American Humorist & Lecturer)
乔希·比林斯（美国幽默作家、讲师）

The devotee is entirely free to criticize; the
fanatic can safely be a skeptic. Love is not
blind; that is the last thing that it is. Love is
bound; and the more it is bound the less it
is blind.

——G.K. Chesterton
(British Journalist & Novelist)
切斯特顿（英国记者、小说家）

12

Grow old along with me. The best is yet to be. The last of life, for which the first was made.

——Robert Browning
(British Poet)
罗伯特·布朗宁（英国诗人）

我能想到最浪漫的事，就是和你一起慢慢变老。一路上收藏点点滴滴的欢笑，留到以后坐着摇椅慢慢聊；直到我们老的哪儿也去不了，你还依然把我当成手心里的宝。

——姚若龙（词作家）
《最浪漫的事》
Yao Ruolong (Lyric Writer)

我怕来不及，我要抱着你，直到感觉你的皱纹有了岁月的痕迹，……
动也不能动，也要看着你，直到感觉你的发线有了白雪的痕迹，……

——林夕（词作家）
《至少还有你》
Lin Xi (Lyric Writer)

死生契阔，与子相悦；
执子之手，与子偕老。

——《诗经》
Chinese Proverb

Love & Marriage　愛情&婚姻

Love is the embracing of nudity.

——Oscar Wilde
(Irish Playwright & Poet)
王尔德（爱尔兰剧作家、诗人）

而那时他想爱情不能总是在表示思念的低音符上徘徊，它需要在高音符上爆发。于是，把闪光的衣衫全脱去，爱情只不过是赤裸裸的肉体相接罢了！

——张贤亮（作家）
《习惯死亡》
Zhang Xianliang (Author)

Without respect, love cannot go far.

——Alexander Dumasfils
(French Historical Novelist)
小仲马（法国历史小说家）

相敬如宾。

——春秋·左丘明（史学家）
《左传·僖位公三十三年》
Zuo Qiuming (Historian)

举案齐眉。

——南朝·宋·范晔（史学家）
《后汉书·梁鸿传》
Fan Ye (Historian)

14

浪漫的爱，有一最显著的特点，就是这爱永远处于可望而不可及的地步，永远存在于追求的状态中，永远被视为一种极圣洁极高贵极虚无缥缈的东西。

——梁实秋（学者、翻译家、文学评论家）
《谈徐志摩》
Liang Shiqiu (Scholar, Translator & Critic)

People don't fall in love with what's right in front of them. People want the dream-what they can't have. The more unattainable, the more attractive.

—John Pierce Askegren
(American Author)
约翰·皮尔斯（美国著作家）

Love doesn't just sit there, like a stone; it has to be made, like bread, remade all the time, made new.

——Ursula Kroeber Le Guin
(American Author)
乌尔苏拉·克罗伯·勒·吉恩（美国著作家）

爱情必须时时更新，生长，创造。

——鲁迅（文学家、思想家、革命家）
《彷徨》集之《伤逝》
Lu Xun (Writer, Philosopher & Revolutionist)

爱情的火是跳动的，需要新的燃料，
否则很容易被人世的冷风一下子吹熄了。

——佚名
Anonymous

One ought to hold on to one's heart; for if one lets it go, one soon loses control of the head too.

——Friedrich Wilhelm Nietzsche
(German Philosopher)
尼采（德国哲学家）

爱情犹如洞庭湖里的水波，你要不控制，它会淹没你跟你的一切，你的志向、事业、精力甚至生命。

——周立波（作家）
Zhou Libo (Author)

It is better to have loved and lost, than never to have loved at all.

——Alfred, Lord Tennyson
(English Poet)
丁尼生（英国诗人）

失去总比从来没有过的好一些，因为前者还有甜蜜的回忆与渺茫的期待。

——苏青（小说家、散文家、剧作家）
《谈女人》
Su Qing (Novelist, Essayist & Dramatist)

16

也想不相思，可免相思苦。
几次细思量，情愿相思苦！

——胡适（学者、诗人、哲学家）
Hu Shi (Scholar, Poet & Philosopher)

You can give without loving, but you cannot love without giving.

——Amy Carmichael
(Christian Missionary)
艾米·卡迈克尔(基督传教士)

帮助不等于爱情，
但爱情不能不包括帮助。

——鲁迅(文学家、思想家、革命家)
Lu Xun (Writer, Philosopher & Revolutionist)

在感情上，当你想征服对方的时候，实际上已经在一定程度上被对方征服了。首先是对方对你的吸引，然后才是你征服对方的欲望。

——汪国真(诗人)
Wang Guozhen (Poet)

When a young man complains that a young lady has no heart, it is pretty certain sign that she has his.

——George Dennison Prentice
(American Journalist)
乔治·丹尼森·普伦蒂斯(美国记者)

You think that you are Ann's suitor: that you are the pursuer and she the pursued...Fool: it is you who are the pursued, the marked down quarry, the destined prey.

——George Bernard Shaw
萧伯纳(爱尔兰剧作家)

Love & Marriage　　爱情&婚姻

Jealously is always born with love but it does not die with it.

——Francois de La Rochefoucauld
(French Novelist & Playwright)
拉罗什福科（法国小说家、剧作家）

有爱必有妒。

——林语堂（学者、文学家、语言学家）
Lin Yutang (Scholar, Writer & Linguist)

问题不在于找一个全无缺点的对象，而是要找一个双方缺点都能认识，各自承认、愿意逐渐改，同时能彼此容忍的伴侣。

——傅雷（翻译家、作家、文学评论家）
Fu Lei (Translator, Author & Critic)

We all have a childhood dream that when there is love, everything goes like silk, but the reality is that marriage requires a lot of compromise.

——Raquel Welch
(Golden Globe Winning American Actress)
拉奎尔·韦尔奇（美国金球奖获奖演员）

A good marriage is the union of two good forgivers.

——Ruth Bell Graham
(American Philanthropist & wife of Evangelist Billy Graham)
路得·贝尔·格兰汉姆（美国慈善家、布道者比利·格兰汉姆之妻）

18

Nobody's sweetheart is ugly.

——Jean Joseph Vade
(French Song Writer)
约瑟夫·瓦迪(法国作曲家)

情人眼裡出西施。

——清·翟灏(艺术家)
《能人编·妇女》
Zhai Hao (Artist)

Beauty is bought by judgment of the eye.

——William Shakespeare
(English Dramatist)
莎士比亚(英国剧作家)

Beauty in things exists in the mind which contemplates them.

——David Hume
(Scottish Philosopher)
休谟(英国哲学家)

Beauty is in the eye of the beholder.

——Margaret Wolfe Hungerford
(Irish Novelist)
玛格丽特·沃尔夫·亨格福德(爱尔兰小说家)

Love & Marriage　　愛情&婚姻

商场得意，情场失意。

——谚语
Chinese Proveb

When success comes in the door, it seems, love often goes out the window.

——Joyce Brothers
(American Psychologist)
乔伊斯·卜洛泽(美国心理学家)

小别胜新婚。

——谚语
Chinese Proveb

Absence is to love what wind is to fire;
it extinguishes the small, and inflames the great.

——Roger de Bussy Rabutin
(French Soldier & Writer)
罗杰·德·比西·拉比旦(法国军人、作家)

Absence makes the heart grow fonder.

——Thomas Haynes Bayly
(English Poet)
托马斯·黑恩·贝理(英国诗人)

Temporary parting deepens love, while separating strangles love.

——Bortolt Brecht
(German Dramatist & Poet)
布莱希特(德国戏剧家、诗人)

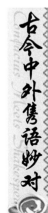

Chapter 3

Beauty soon grows familiar to the lover, fades in his eye, and palls upon the sense.

——Joseph Addison
(English Essayist & Poet)
约瑟夫·阿狄森（英国散文家、诗人）

21

入芝兰之室，久而不闻其香。

——春秋·鲁·孔子（思想家、教育家）
《孔子家语·六本》
Confucius (Philosopher & Educator)

Marriage happens as with cages: the birds without despair to get in, and those within despair of getting out.

——Montaigne
(French Philosopher & Essayist)
蒙田（法国哲学家、散文家）

围在城里的人想逃出来，城外的人想冲进去。对婚姻也罢，职业也罢，人生的愿望大都如此。

——钱钟书（作家、文学研究家）
《围城》
Qian Zhongshu (Author)

On Marriage   婚姻

Relationship is like a bank account we must invest to withdrawal.

——John C. Maxwell
(American Leadership Trainer)
约翰·麦克斯威尔（美国领导教练）

爱情就如在银行里存一笔钱，
能欣赏对方的优点，这是补充收入；
容忍缺点，这是节制支出。

——沈君山（教授）
Shen Junshan (Professor)

Dutiful roses are a contradiction in terms. If I am not moved by a spontaneous affection for her as a person, the roses do not honor her. In fact, they belittle her.

——Max Lucado
(America Christian Author)
陆可铎（美国畅销童书作家）

只为道德去爱一个人，可能是一种缺陷；而不顾道德去爱一个人，只可能是一场悲剧。

——丁凯隆（作家）
《爱与美之歌》
Ding Kailong (Author)

Open both eyes before marriage, half shut afterwards.

——Benjamin Franklin
(American Statesman & Scientist)
富兰克林（美国政治家、科学家）

婚姻生活者，半睁眼半闭眼的生活也。天下没有十全十美的男女，如果眼睛睁得太久，或用照妖镜照得太久，恐怕连上帝身上都能挑出毛病。

——柏杨（学者、作家） Bai Yang (Scholar & Author)

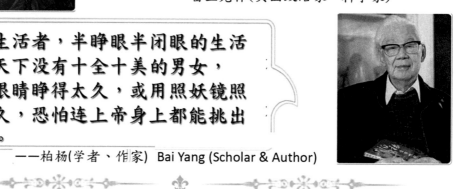

God the best maker of all marriages, combine your hearts in one.

——William Shakespeare
(English Dramatist)
莎士比亚（英国剧作家）

千里姻缘一线牵。

——唐•李复言（小说家）
《续玄怪录》
Li Fuyan (Novelist)

从来说月下老赤绳系足，虽千里之外，到底相合。

——明•凌蒙初（小说家）
《初刻拍案惊奇》
Ling Mengchu (Novelist)

On Marriage　婚姻

身无彩凤双飞翼，
心有灵犀一点通。

——唐·李商隐(诗人)
《无题》其一
Li Shangyin (Poet)

Two souls with but a single thought,
two hearts that beat as one.

——Friedrich Halm
(Austrian Dramatist)
弗里德里希·哈尔姆(奥地利戏剧作家)

Two souls turn into one mind. Two hearts
share one body.

——Fridtjof Nansen
(Norwegian Polar Explorer)
弗里德约夫·南森(挪威极地探险家)

24

Two friends—two bodies with one
soul inspired.

——Homer
(Greek Epic Poet)
荷马(希腊史诗诗人)

Love keeps no record of wrongs.

——Bible
《圣经》

夫妻吵嘴不记仇。
床头打架床尾和。

——俗语
Chinese Proveb

夫妻没有隔夜仇。
天上下雨地下流，小两口儿打架不记仇。

——俗语
Chinese Proveb

A happy marriage is the union of two good forgivers.

——Ruth Bell Graham

路得·贝尔·格兰汉姆

Horses (thou say'st) and asses men may try, And ring suspected vessels ere they buy; But wives, a random choice, untried they take; they dream in courtship but in wedlock wake.

——Alexander Pope
(English Poet)
亚历山大·蒲柏（英国诗人）

买锅要敲打， 娶嫁要细查。

——谚语
Chinese Proveb

The first half of life consists of the capacity to enjoy without the chance; the last half consists of the chance without the capacity.

——Mark Twain
(American Novelist)
马克·吐温(美国小说家)

人生得意须尽欢，
莫使金樽空对月。

——唐·李白(浪漫主义诗人)
《将进酒》
Li Bai (Poet)

A tragic irony of life is that we so often achieve success or financial independence after the chief reason for which we sought it has passed away.

——Edward Judson
(American Writer)
爱德华·贾德森(美国作家)

劝君莫惜金缕衣，劝君惜取少年时。
花开堪折直须折，莫待无花空折枝。

——唐•杜秋娘(歌妓、唐宪宗宠妃)
《金缕衣》
Du Qiuniang (Geisha & Imperial Concubine)

行乐须及春。

——唐·李白(浪漫主义诗人)
《月下独酌》
Li Bai (Poet)

On Life　　人生

Like our shadows, our wishes lengthen as our sun declines.

——Edward Young
(English Poet)
爱德华·杨（英国诗人）

夕阳无限好，只是近黄昏。

——唐·李商隐（诗人）
《登乐游原》
Li Shangyin (Poet)

天生我才必有用。

——唐·李白（浪漫主义诗人）
《将进酒》
Li Bai (Poet)

No man is useless in this world who lightens the burden of someone else.

——Charles Dickens
(English Novelist)
狄更斯（英国小说家）

Every human being is intended to have a character of his own; to be what no others are, and to do what no other can do.

——William Ellery Channing
(American Poet)
威廉·钱宁（美国诗人）

28

Time is like that surging rapids, going away mercilessly without returning.

——Miguel de Cervantes
(Spanish Novelist & Poet)
塞万提斯（西班牙小说家、诗人）

人生天地之间，若白驹之过卻，忽然而已。

——战国·宋·庄子（思想家、哲学家、文学家）
《庄子·知北游》
Zhuangzi (Philosopher & Writer)

聪明的你，告诉我，我们的日子为什么一去不复返呢？——是有人偷了他们罢：那是谁？又藏在何处呢？是他们自己逃走了罢：现在又到了哪里呢？过去的日子如轻烟，被微风吹散了，如薄雾，被初阳蒸融了。

——朱自清（作家、学者）
《匆匆》
Zhu Ziqing (Author & Scholar)

乐极生悲。

——西汉·淮南王·刘安（思想家、文学家）
《淮南子·道应训》
Liu An (Philosopher & Writer)

Sometimes you can get a splinter even sliding down a rainbow.

——Cherralea Morgen

On Life　　人生

If you do not bring Paris with you, you will not find it there.

——John M. Shanahan
约翰·M·沙纳汉

犹似风景之美不在其中而在其外。

——丰子恺（艺术家、文学家、翻译家）
Feng Zikai (Artist, Writer & Translator)

祸兮福之所倚，福兮祸之所伏。

——春秋·西周·老子（哲学家、思想家）
Laozi (Philosopher)

Even in laughter the heart may ache, and joy may end in grief.

——Dan Steve Carlson
(American Pitcher)
丹·史蒂夫·卡尔森（美国投手）

Prosperity is not without many fears and disasters, and adversity is not without comforts and hopes.

——Francis Bacon
(English Philosopher & Scientist)
培根（英国哲学家、科学家）

> In heaven all is gladness. In hell all is sorrow. Upon this earth, since it lies between, sometimes the one, and sometimes the other. We have our being between the two extremes, and so it partakes of both. Fortune should vary, not all being felicity, nor all adversity.

——Baltasar Gracian
(Spanish Prose Writer)
巴尔塔沙·葛拉西安（西班牙散文作家）

> 人有悲欢离合，月有阴晴圆缺，此事古难全。

——北宋·苏轼（词人、书画家）
《水调歌头》
Su Shi (Poet & Painter-calligrapher)

> 祸不单行。

——西汉·刘向（文学家）
《说苑·权谋》
Liu Xiang (Writer)

> When sorrows come, they come not as a single spy but in battalions.

——William Shakespeare
(English Dramatist)
莎士比亚（英国剧作家）

> Misery loves company.

——John Ray
(English Naturalist)
雷·约翰（英国博物学家）

\ *On Life*   人生

Equality of opportunity is an equal opportunity to prove unequal talents.

——Viscount Samuel
(Peerage of the United Kingdom)
塞缪尔子爵（英国贵族）

给你比赛的场地，帮你明确比赛的目标，将比赛的规则公开化，谁能跑在前面，就看你自己的了。

——张瑞敏（海尔集团董事局主席兼CEO）
Zhang Ruimin (Econimist, Bussiness Man)

子曰：吾十有五而志于学，三十而立，四十而不惑，五十而知天命，六十而耳顺，七十而从心所欲，不逾矩。

——春秋·鲁·孔子（思想家、教育家）
Confucius (Philosopher & Educator)

At twenty, a man is a peacock, at thirty a lion, at forty a camel, at fifty a serpent, at sixty a dog, at seventy an ape, and at eighty, nothing at all.

——Baltasar Gracian
(Spanish Prose Writer)
巴尔塔沙·葛拉西安（西班牙散文作家）

At twenty years of age, the will reigns; at thirty, the wit; and at forty, the judgment.

——Benjamin Franklin
(American Statesman & Scientist)
富兰克林（美国政治家、科学家）

32

古今中外隽语妙对

By medicine life may be prolonged, yet death will seize the doctor too.

——William Shakespeare
(English Dramatist)
莎士比亚（英国剧作家）

能医不自医。

——谚语
Chinese Proverb

One bad move nullifies forty good ones.

--Al Horowitz
(Chess master)
棋術專家

一着不慎，满盘皆输。

——谚语
Chinese Proverb

一子错，满盘皆落索。

——俗语
Chinese Proverb

小心驶得万年船。

——成语
Chinese Proverb

On Life   人生

All my best thoughts were stolen by the ancients.

——Ralph Waldo Emerson
(American Philosopher & Writer)
爱默生（美国哲学家、文学家）

莫道君行早，更有早行人。

——《增广贤文》
Chinese Proverb

All men are like grass, and all their glory is like the flowers of the field.

——Bible
《圣经》

人生一回，花艳一季。

——谚语
Chinese Proverb

Don't bother bother till bother bothers you.

——Proverb
西方谚语

烦恼不寻人，人自寻烦恼。

——谚语
Chinese Proverb

祸福无门，唯人所召。

——春秋·鲁·左丘明（史学家）
《左传·襄公二十三年》
Zuo Qiuming (Historian)

Chapter 5

Think like a man of action, and act like a man of thought.

——Henri Bergson
(French Philosopher)
亨利·柏格森(法国哲学家)

知行合一。

——明·王阳明(思想家、哲学家、军事家)
Wang Yangming (Philosopher & Militarist)

Sloth wears faster than rust consumes.

——Benjamin Franklin
(American Statesman & Scientist)
富兰克林(美国政治家、科学家)

人同机器一样，
经常运动才不会生锈。

——朱德(军事家)
Zhu De (Militarist)

35

A rolling stone gathers no moss.

——Publilius Syrus
(Assyrian Latin Writer of Maxims)
希如斯（叙利亚-拉丁格言作家）

流水不腐，户枢不蠹。

——战国·吕不韦（商人、政治家、思想家）
《吕氏春秋·尽数》
Lv Buwei (Businessman, Politician & Philoopher)

A thought which does not result in an action is nothing much, and an action which does not proceed from a thought is nothing at all.

——Georges Bernanos
(French Author)
乔治·贝纳诺斯（法国作家）

36

知者行之始，行者知之成。

——明·王阳明（思想家、哲学家、军事家）
Wang Yangming (Philosopher & Militarist)

古今中外隽语妙对

Upon the stars, but more upon effort, for while the former give birth, the latter brings development; great gifts are not enough, even when they exist, but he easily finds the way, who has found the will.

——Baltasar Gracian
(Spanish Prose Writer)
巴尔塔沙·葛拉西安

有其志必成其事。

——三国·魏·曹操(军事家、政治家、诗人)
Cao Cao (Militarist, Politician & Poet)

有志者事竟成。

——南朝·宋·范晔(史学家)
《后汉书·耿弇传》
Fan Ye (Historian)

"Where there is a will, there is a way. If there is a chance in a million that you can do something, anything, to keep what you want from ending, do it. Pry the door open or, if need be, wedge your foot in that door and keep it open."

Pauline Kael (American Film Critic)
宝琳·凯尔(美国影评家)

On Action   行动

天下难事必做于易，
天下大事必做于细。

——春秋·西周·老子(哲学家、思想家)
《道德经》
Laozi (Philosopher)

Only those who have the patience to do simple things perfectly ever acquire the skill to do difficult things easily.

——Friedrich von Schiller
(German Dramatist & Poet)
席勒(德国剧作家、诗人)

I long to accomplish a great and noble task, but it is my chief duty to accomplish small tasks as if they were great and noble.

——Helen Keller
(American Blind & Deaf Writer)
海伦·凯勒(美国盲聋女作家)

38

To succeed in a great cause, one must begin from the trivialities.

——Vladimir Ilich Lenin
(Founder of Russian Soviet Socialist Republic)
列宁(苏维埃社会主义共和国创始人)

The never-ending flight of future days.

——John Milton
(British Poet)
约翰·弥尔顿（英国诗人）

今日复今日，今日何其少！
今日又不为，此事何时了？

——明·文嘉（诗人、书画家）
《今日歌》
Wen Jia (Poet & Painter-calligrapher)

Never put off till tomorrow, what you can do today.

——Lord Chesterfield
(British Statesman, Diplomat & Wit)
切斯特菲尔德爵士（英国政治家、外交家、智者）

明日复明日，明日何其多！
我生待明日，万事成蹉跎。

——明·文嘉（诗人、书画家）
《明日歌》
Wen Jia (Poet & Painter-calligrapher)

将来的事，将来再说；
现在有路，现在先走！

——茅盾（文学家）
Mao Dun (Writer)

On Action 行动

With the past, I have nothing to do; nor with the future. I live now.

——Ralph Waldo Emerson
(American Philosopher & Writer)
爱默生(美国哲学家、文学家)

过去的，让它过去，永远不要回顾；
未来的，等来了时再说，不要空想；
我们只抓住了现在，用我们现在的理
想，做我们所应该做的。

——茅盾(文学家)
Mao Dun (Writer)

I try to learn from the past, but I plan for the future by focusing exclusively on the present. That's where the fun is.

——Donald John Trump
(American Businessman)
唐纳德·川普(美国商人)

The past cannot be regained, although we can learn from it; the future is not yet ours even though we must plan for it. Time is now. We have only today.

——Charles E. Hummel
(Former President of Barrington College)
查尔斯·胡梅尔(美国巴林顿大学前任校长)

No longer forward nor behind I look In hope or fear; but grateful, take the good I find, the best of now and here.

——John Greenleaf Whittier
(American Quaker Poet)
约翰·林格利夫·惠帝尔(美国诗人)

40

Jack of all trades, master of none.

——Proverb
西方谚语

件件都能，其实也就是一无所长。

——杨绛（翻译家、剧作家）
Yang Jiang (Translator & Dramatist)

无所不能的人实在是一无所能，无所不专的专家
实在是一无所专。

——邹韬奋(政论家、出版家)
(Political Commentator & Publisher)

十事半通，不如一事精通。

——谚语
Chinese Proverb

教之道，贵以专。

——《三字经》
Chinese Proverb

Unreasonable haste is the direct road to error.

——Moliere
(French Playwright)
（莫里哀法国作家）

What is made in haste is unmade as soon; and what is to last an eternity, may well tarry another in its creation.

——Baltasar Gracian
(Spanish Baroque Prose Writer)
巴尔塔沙·葛拉西安（西班牙散文作家）

欲速则不达。

——《论语·子路》
Confucius (Philosopher & Educator)

Stuck between a rock and a hard place.

——Proverb
西方谚语

42

进退维谷

——诗经
Chinese Proverb

When one door closes, another opens; but we often look so long and so regretfully upon the closed door that we do not see the one which has opened for us.

——Alexander Graham Bell
(British Inventor)
亚历山大·格兰汉姆·贝尔（英国发明家）

43

东方不亮西方亮，黑了南方有北方。

——毛泽东
（革命家、中国共产党、新中国领导人）
Mao Zedong (Revolutionist & Communist)

I will not just live my life. I will not just spend my life. I will invest my life.

——Helen Keller
(American Blind & Deaf Writer)
海伦·凯勒（美国盲聋女作家）

人的生命是有限的，可是，为人民服务是无限的，我要把有限的生命，投入到无限的为人民服务之中去。

——雷锋（军人）
Lei Feng (Soldier)

On Happiness, Ideal 幸福与理想

I would sooner fail than not be ranked with the greatest.

——John Keats
(English Poet)
约翰·济慈（英国诗人）

生当作人杰，死亦为鬼雄。

—— 南宋·李清照（女词人）
《夏日绝句》
Li Qingzhao (Poet)

You can only come to the morning through the shadows.

—— J.R.R. Tolkien (English Writer)
托尔金 （英国作家）

44

光明的前夜，常有暂时的黑暗。

——徐特立（革命家、教育家）
Xu Teli (Revolutionist & Educator)

For what is a man? What has he got?
If not himself - Then he has naught.
To say the things he truly feels
And not the words of one who kneels.
The record shows I took the blows
And did it my way.
Yes, it was my way.

——Frank Sinatra
(American Singer & Actor)
弗兰克·西纳特拉(美国歌唱家、演员)

不管成功还是失败，
我有我的方向。

——张艺谋(导演、摄影师、演员)
Zhang Yimou (Director, Camerist & Actor)

Be happy. It's one way of being wise.

——Colette aka Sidonie Gabrielle
(French National Treasure Writer)
西多妮·加布里埃尔·科莱特(法国国宝级女作家)

福至心灵。

——宋·毕仲洵(翰林学士)
《幕府燕闲录》
Bi Zhongxun (Scholar)

百尺竿头，更进一步。

——北宋·释道元
《景德传灯录》
Shi Daoyuan

Swifter, Higher, Stronger.

——Olympic Motto
奥林匹克格言

On Happiness, Ideal 幸福与理想

Simplicity, clarity, singleness: these are the attributes that give our lives power and vividness and joy.

——Richard Holloway
(Scottish Writer)
理查德·霍洛韦（苏格兰作家）

见素抱朴，少私寡欲。

——春秋·西周·老子（哲学家、思想家）
Laozi (Philosopher)

别人先苦后甜，那甜特甜。我十六岁成名，是先甜后苦，那苦特苦。

——钟镇涛（歌星、演员）
Zhong Zhentao (Singer & Actor)

For in all adversity of fortune the worst sort of misery is to have been happy.

——Anicius Manlius Severinus Boëthius
(Ancient Rome Philosopher)
波伊提乌（古罗马哲学家）

The bitter must come before the sweet; and that also will make the sweet the sweeter.

——John Bunyan
(English Christian Writer)
约翰·班扬（英国基督教作家）

46

古今中外隽语妙对

To see a world in a grain of sand and a heaven in a wild flower, hold infinity in the palm of your hand and eternity in an hour.

——William Blake
(English Poet & Painter)
威廉·布莱克（英国诗人、画家）

心若无尘，一花一世界，一鸟一天堂。
心若无尘，一叶一菩提，一土一如来。
心若无尘，一方一净土，一笑一尘缘。
心若无尘，一念一清静，心是莲花开。

——佛经
Suatra

The very first condition of lasting happiness is that a life should be full of purpose, aiming at something outside self.

——Hugo Lafayette Black
(American Politician & Jurist)
雨果·拉斐特·布莱克（美国政治家、法理学家）

助人为快乐之本。

——谚语
Chinese Proveb

Do I not kill an enemy when I turn them into a friend?

——Abraham Lincoln
(16th President of the United States)
林肯（美国第十六任总统

化干戈为玉帛。

——西汉·淮南王·刘安（思想家、文学家）
《淮南子·原道训》
Liu An (Philosopher & Writer)

Fear less, hope more; eat less, chew more,; whine less, breathe more; talk less, say more; hate less, love more; and all good things are yours.

——Swedish Proverb
瑞典谚语

少肉多菜；少盐多醋；
少糖多果；少食多嚼；
少衣多浴；少车多步；
少忧多眠；少怒多笑；
少言多行；少欲多施。

48

——健康十训
Chinese Proverb

Chapter 7

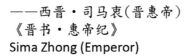

> Poverty is an abnormality to rich people. It is very difficult to make out why people who want dinner do not ring the bell.

——Walter Bagehot
(British Economist, Essayist & Journalist)
白芝浩(英国经济学家、评论家、记者)

何不吃肉糜？

——西晋·司马衷(晋惠帝)
《晋书·惠帝纪》
Sima Zhong (Emperor)

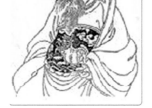

有钱能使鬼推磨。

——西晋·鲁褒(文学家)
《钱神论》
Lu Bao (Writer)

> I see no point in money except to buy off anxiety. I don't want to be rich. I want to be unanxious.

——Sir John Betjeman
(British Poet)
约翰·贝杰曼爵士(英国诗人)

> Money is good for bribing yourself through the inconveniences of life.

——Gottfried Reinhardt
(German Film Director)
莱因哈特(德国电影导演)

Wealth and Money 财富

Offense is easy, defense is work.

——Phil Jackson
(American Basketball Coach)
菲尔·杰克逊（美国篮球教练）

打江山易，守江山难。

——北宋·司马光（政治家、文学家、史学家）
《资治通鉴·唐纪》
Sima Guang (Politician, Writer & Historian)

To acquire wealth is difficult, to preserve it more difficult.

——Day, Edmund Ezra
(American Economist & Educator)
埃德蒙·以斯拉（美国经济学家、教育家）

创业难，守业更难。

——清·吴敬梓（小说家）
《儒林外史》
Wu Jingzi (Novelist)

战胜易，守胜难。

——战国·卫·吴起（军事家）
《吴子兵法》
Wu Qi (Militarist)

50

古今中外隽语妙对

If thou covet riches, ask not but for contentment, which is an immense treasure.

——Sa'Di
(Medieval Persian Poet)
萨迪（中世纪波斯诗人）

知足者富

——春秋·西周·老子（哲学家、思想家）
《道德经》
Laozi (Philosopher)

知足之足，恒足矣。

——春秋·西周·老子（哲学家、思想家）
《道德经》
Laozi (Philosopher)

My crown is called content, a crown that seldom kings enjoy.

——William Shakespeare
(English Dramatist)
莎士比亚（英国剧作家）

Having the fewest wants, I am nearest to the gods.

——Socrates
(Ancient Greek Philosopher)
苏格拉底（古希腊哲学家）

Wealth and Money 财富

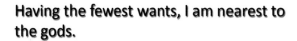

Having been poor is no shame, but being ashamed if it is.

——Benjamin Franklin
(American Statesman & Scientist)
富兰克林（美国政治家、科学家）

子曰：士志于道，而耻恶衣恶食者，未足与议也！

——春秋·孔子（思想家、教育家）
《论语》
Confucius (Philosopher & Educator)

The greatest of evils and the worst of crimes is poverty; our first duty—a duty to which every other consideration should be sacrificed—is not to be poor.

——George Bernard Shaw
(Irish Playwright)
萧伯纳（爱尔兰剧作家）

52

就整个社会而言，贫就是病。

——梁实秋（学者、翻译家、文学评论家）
Liang Shiqiu (Scholar, Translator & Critic)

As always, victory finds a hundred fathers, but defeat is an orphan.

——Count Galeazzo Ciano
(Italian Minister of Foreign Affairs)
亚佐·齐亚诺伯爵(前意大利外交部长)

贫居闹市无人问， 富在深山有远亲。

——《增广贤文》
Chinese Proverb

人生万事无缘足，待足是何时？

——南宋·黄机(词人)
《眼儿媚》
Huang Ji (Poet)

When you are skinning your customers you should leave some skin on to grow so that you can skin them again.

——Nikita Khrushchev
(General Secretary of the
Communist Party of the Soviet Union)
赫鲁晓夫 (俄国 共产主义部长)

焚林而田，偷取多兽，后必无兽。

——战国•韩非子
(哲学家、思想家、政论家、散文家)
《韩非子•难一》
Han Feizi
(Philosopher, Political Commentator & Essayist)

Money can buy medicine, but not health.
Money can buy a house, but not a home.
Money can buy companionship, but not friends.
Money can buy entertainment, but not happiness.
Money can buy a bed, but not sleep.
Money can buy books, but not brains.
Money can buy finery, but not beauty.
Money can buy a crucifix, but not a Savior.
Money can buy "the good life," but not eternal life.
As Seneca, the Roman statesman, once said, "money has never yet made anyone rich."

——Henry Gariepy
(American Editor)

亨利·嘉瑞彼
（美国编辑）

钱能买来纸醉金迷，能买来楼台美人，但买不来尊严和爱。

——老愚(作家)
Lao Yu (Writer)

"Money will buy you a fine dog, but only love can make it wag its tail"

——Kinky Friedman
(American Songwriter)
金利·弗里德曼
（美国歌曲作家）

If you sell the cow, you sell her milk too.

——Proverb
西方谚语

竭泽而渔…而明年无鱼。

《吕氏春秋·孝行览·义赏》
Lu Buwei (Businessman, Politician & Philosopher)

Chapter 8

If there is any great secret of success in life, it lies in the ability to put yourself in the other person's place and to see things from his point of view—as well as your own.

——Henry Ford
(American Industrialist)
亨利·福特（美国实业家）

将心比心。

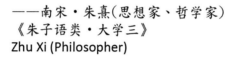

——南宋·朱熹（思想家、哲学家）
《朱子语类·大学三》
Zhu Xi (Philosopher)

Genius is one percent inspiration and ninety-nine percent perspiration.

——Albert Einstein
(German Theoretical Physicist)
爱因斯坦（德国理论物理学家）

天才在某种程度上是汗水的结晶物。

——秦牧（文学家）
Qin Mu (Writer)

一个商人要在经验中成熟，其中刻苦耐劳占了百分之九十五。

——霍英东（企业家）
Huo Yingdong (Entrepreneur)

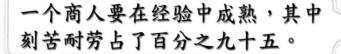

On Success　　成功

It takes twenty years to make an overnight success.

——Eddie Cantor
(American Comedian)
埃迪·康托尔（美国喜剧演员）

十年寒窗无人问，
一举成名天下知。

——元·高明（作家）
《琵琶记》
Gao Ming (Author)

Do not be deceived, God is not mocked, for whatever a man sows, that he will also reap.

——St. Paul
(Apostle of Jesus)
圣保罗（耶稣的使徒）

种牡丹者得花，种蒺藜者得刺。

——鲁迅（文学家、思想家、革命家）
《答有恒先生》
Lu Xun (Writer, Philosopher & Revolutionist)

尽一分之心力，必有一分之补益。
故惟日孜孜，但以造因为事，则他
日结果之收成，必有不可量者。

——梁启超（政治家、学者）
《成败》
Liang Qichao (Politician & Scholar)

56

It is literally true that you can succeed best and quickest by helping others to succeed.

——Napoleon Hill
(American Self Help Author)
拿破仑·希尔（美国自助作者）

助人则自助。

——恽代英（无产阶级革命家）
Yun Daiying (Revolutionist)

No man can live happily who regards himself alone; who turns everything to his own advantage. You must live for others if you wish to live for yourself.

——Lucius Annaeus Seneca
(Roman Orator & Writer)
塞内卡（罗马演说家、作家）

要照顾对方的利益，这样人家才愿与你合作，并希望下一次合作。

——李嘉诚（企业家、慈善家）
Li Jiaocheng (Businessman & Philanthropist)

处世让一步为高，退步即进步的张本；待人宽一分是福，利人实利己的根基。

——明·洪应明（作家）
《菜根谭》
Hong Yingming (Author)

On Success　　成功

Soldiers generally win battles and generals get the credit for them.

——Napoleon Bonaparte
(French Military & Political Leader)
拿破仑（法国军事、政治领导人）

一将功成万骨枯。

——晚唐·曹松（诗人）
《己亥岁二首》其一
Cao Song (Poet)

Try not to become a man of success but rather try to become a man of value.

——Albert Einstein
(German Theoretical Physicist)
爱因斯坦（德国理论物理学家）

人要做有用的人，不要做只讲体面，
而对别人没有好处的人。

——许地山（作家、学者）
《落花生》
Xu Dishan (Author & Scholar)

58

人要立志做大事，不要立志做大官

——孙中山（近代中国的民主革命家）
Sun Zhongshan (Revolutionist)

The dictionary is the only place that success comes before work. Hard work is the price we must pay for success. I think you can accomplish anything if you're willing to pay the price.

——Vincent Thomas Lombardi
(American Football Coach)
文森特·托马斯·隆巴迪（美式足球教练）

不付出血汗，希冀成绩会从天而降，那是幻想。

——苏步青（数学家）
Su Buqing (Mathmatician)

Nothing is impossible to a willing heart.

——Thomas Heywood
(English Dramatist)
托马斯·海伍德（英国剧作家）

有志者事竟成也。

——南朝·宋·范晔（史学家）
《后汉书·耿弇传》
Fan Ye (Historian)

绳锯木断，水滴石穿。

——南宋·罗大经（文学家）
《鹤林玉露》
Luo Dajing (Writer)

A strong passion for any object will ensure success, for the desire of the end will point out the means.

——William Hazlitt (British Essayist)
威廉·哈兹里特（英国散文家）

天下无难事，只怕有心人。

——明·王骥德（戏曲作家）
《韩夫人题红记·花阴私祝》
Wang Jide (Dramatist)

只要功夫深，铁杵磨成针。

——南宋·祝穆（词人）
《方舆胜览·眉州·磨针溪》
Zhu Mu (Poet)

60

冰冻三尺，非一日之寒。

——东汉·王充（思想家）
《论衡·壮留》
Wang Chong (Philosopher)

If I have seen further it is only by standing on the shoulders of giants.

——Isaac Newton
(English Philosopher & Scientist)
牛顿（英国哲学家、科学家）

会当凌绝顶，一览众山小。

——唐·杜甫（现实主义诗人）
《望岳》
Du Fu (Poet)

No great man ever complains of want of opportunity.

——Ralph Waldo Emerson
(American Philosopher & Writer)
爱默生（美国哲学家、文学家）

机会，是经常出现的。然而，对于那些胸无大志的人来说，机会总是从他们的手指缝中溜掉。其实，没有机会只是弱者的推脱之词。

——李燕杰（演讲家、教育家）
Li Yanjie (Lecturer & Educator)

If you should put even a little on a little, and should do this often, soon this too would become big.

——Hesiod
(Greek Oral Poet)
赫西奥德(希腊口头诗人)

无数的沙砾积成一座山丘，每粒沙都有同等造山的功绩。

——曹禺(戏剧家)
《日出》
Cao Yu (Dramatist)

积土成山，积水成渊。

——战国·赵·荀子(思想家、政治家)
《荀子·劝学》
Xunzi (Philosopher & Politician)

Rome was not built in a day.

——John Heywood
(English Poet)
约翰·海伍德(英国诗人)

积少成多。

——《战国策·秦策四》
Chinese Proverb

聚沙成塔。

——《妙法莲华经·方便品》
Chinese Proverb

When written in Chinese, the word "crisis" is composed of two characters. One represents danger and the other represents opportunity.

——John F. Kennedy
(35th President of the United States)
约翰·F.肯尼迪(美国第三十五任总统)

Danger will wink on opportunity.

——John Milton
(British Poet)
约翰·弥尔顿(英国诗人)

Trouble is only opportunity in work clothes.

——Henry John Kaiser
(American Industrialist)
亨利·凯泽(美国实业家)

危机，危机，有危才有机。

——常用语
Chinese Proverb

Inside my empty bottle I was constructing a lighthouse while all the others were making ships.

——Charles Simic
(Serbian-American Poet)
查尔斯·西米奇(塞尔维亚裔美国诗人)

当别人都在摘橘子的时候，就是该卖篮子的时候了。

—— 臧昱卓
Frank Tsang (C.E.O. USLawChina)

时势造英雄。

——冰心（诗人、作家、翻译家）
《去国》
Bing Xin (Poet, Author & Translator)

The time produces a President.

——Abraham Lincoln
(16th President of the United States)
林肯（美国第十六任总统）

Nay, in every epoch of the world, the great event, parent of all others, is it not the arrival of a Thinker in the world?

——Thomas Carlyle
(British Essayist & Historian)
托马斯·卡莱尔（苏格兰散文家、历史学家）

64

A great epoch calls for great men.

——Proverb
西方谚语

If you run after two hares you will catch neither.

——Proverb
西方谚语

A donkey between two bundles of hay starves.

——Proverb
西方谚语

Between two stools one falls to the ground.

——Proverb
西方谚语

脚踏两头要落空。

——谚语
Chinese Proveb

Between the cup and the lip a morsel may slip.

——Proverb
西方谚语

为山九仞，功亏一篑。

——《尚书·旅獒》
Chinese Proverb

功败垂成。

——《晋书·谢玄传论》
Chinese Proverb

He who fights and runs away may lives to fight another day.

——Proverb
西方谚语

The man does better who runs from disaster than he who is caught by it.

——Homer
(Greek Epic Poet)

三十六计，走为上策。

——南朝·梁·萧子显（史学家）
《南齐书·王敬则传》
Xiao Zixian (Historian)

What comes around goes around.

——Proverb
西方谚语

要知前世因，今生受者是；要知后世果，今生作者是。

——俗语
Chinese Proverb

穷则反，终则始，此物之所有。

——战国·庄子（哲学家）
《庄子·则阳》
Zhuangzi (Philosopher & Writer)

Chapter 9

Even a stopped clock is right twice everyday. After some years, it can boast of a long series of successes.

——Marie von Ebner-Eschenbach
(Austrian Writer)
玛丽·冯·埃布纳·埃申巴赫(奥地利作家)

67

智者千虑，必有一失。

——西汉·司马迁(史学家、文学家、思想家)
《史记·淮阴侯列传》
Sima Qian (Historian, Writer & Philosopher)

The greatest lesson in life is to know that even fools are right sometimes.

——Winston Churchill
(British Former Prime Minister & Statesman)
丘吉尔(英国前首相、政治家)

人非圣贤，孰能无过。

——春秋·左丘明(史学家)
《左传·宣公二年》
Zuo Qiuming (Historian)

Failure / Difficulty / Hard Times 失败与逆境

He who has a strong enough why, can almost bear any how.

——Friedrich Wilhelm Nietzsche
(German Philosopher)
尼采（德国哲学家）

…而有了充实的革命精神生活，就算物质生活差些，就算困难大些，也能忍受和克服。

——陶铸（革命家）
Tao Zhu (Revolutionist)

Success and suffering are vitally and organically linked. If you succeed without suffering, it Is because someone suffered for you; if you suffer without succeeding, it is in order that someone else may succeed after you.

——Edward Judson
(American Writer)
爱德华·贾德森（美国作家）

68

前人种树，后人乘凉。

——清·翟灏（艺术家）
《通俗编·俚语对句》
Zhai Hao (Artist)

过而不改，是为过矣。

——春秋·孔子（思想家、教育家）
《论语·卫灵公》
Confucius (Philosopher & Educator)

It is human to err, but it is devilish to remain willfully in error.

——Saint Augustine
(Berber Philosopher & Theologian)
圣·古奥斯丁（柏柏尔哲学家、神学家）

重蹈覆辙。

——南朝·宋·范晔（史学家）
《后汉书·窦武传》
Fan Ye (Historian)

It is only error in judgment to make a mistake, but it shows infirmity of character to adhere to it when discovered.

——Christian Nevell Bovee
(American Author & Lawyer)
博维（美国作家、律师）

天将降大任于斯人也，必先苦其心志，劳其筋骨，饿其体肤，空乏其身，行拂乱其所为，所以动心忍性，曾益其所不能。

——战国·孟子（思想家、哲学家）
《孟子·告子下》
Mengzi (Philosopher)

God uses suffering as a whetstone, to make men sharp with.

——Henry Ward Beecher
(American Clergyman, Social Reformer)
比彻（美国神职人员、社会改革者）

God brings men into deep waters, not to drown them, but to cleanse them.

—— John H. Aughey
(American Christian Pastor)
约翰·H. 奥格黑（美国基督教牧师）

70

All the adversity I've had in my life, all my troubles and obstacles, have strengthened me ... You may not realize it when it happens, but a kick in the teeth may be the best thing in the world for you.

——Walt Disney
(Founder of Disney Land)
沃尔特•迪斯尼(迪斯尼乐园创始人)

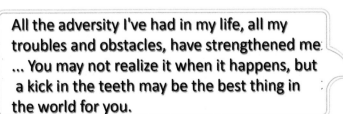

A man is not finished when he's defeated.
He is finished why he quits.

——Richard M. Nixon
(37th President of the United States)
尼克松（美国第三十七任总统）

跌倒不要紧，最要紧是懂得重新站起来。

——杨千嬅（歌星）
Yang Qianhua (Singer)

工欲善其事，必先利其器。

——春秋·孔子（思想家、教育家）
《论语·卫灵公》
Confucius (Philosopher & Educator)

Work with good tools. The excellence of a servant has never dulled the splendor of the master: for all the glory of what is accomplished later descends upon the first cause, as, in reveres, all the disgrace.

——Baltasar Gracian 巴尔塔沙·葛拉西安（西班牙散文作家）

Give me six hours to chop down a tree and I will spend the first four sharpening the axe.

——Abraham Lincoln
(16th President of the United States)
林肯（美国第十六任总统）

Failure / Difficulty / Hard Times 失败与逆境

We are not yet out of the woods, but we can see the glimmers of lights.

——Burnham
(American Architect)
伯纳姆(美国建筑师)

山重水复疑无路，
柳暗花明又一村。

——南宋·陆游(诗人)
《游山西村》
Lu You (Poet)

It's better to strive for the future than to regret the past.

——Karl Marx
(German Political Theorist)
马克思(德国政治理论家)

与其临渊羡鱼，不如退而结网。

——东汉·班固(史学家)
《汉书·董仲舒传》
Ban Gu (Historian)

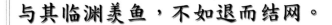

亡羊补牢，未为晚也。

——《战国策》
Chinese Idiom

古今中外隽语妙对

Provide for the worst, the best will save itself.

——Thomas Heywood
(English Dramatist)
托马斯·海伍德（英国剧作家）

居安思危，思则有备，
有备无患，敢以此规。

——春秋·左丘明（史学家）
《左传·襄公十一年》
Zuo Qiuming (Historian)

Poverty sits by the cradle of all our great men and rocks all of them to manhood.

——Heinrich Heine
(German Romantic Poet)
海涅（德国浪漫诗人）

吃得苦中苦，方为人上人。

——明·冯梦龙（文学家）
《警世通言·玉堂春落难逢夫》
Feng Menglong (Writer)

穷人的孩子早当家。

——谚语
Chinese Proverb

Failure / Difficulty / Hard Times 失败与逆境

If it were not for hopes, the heart would break .

——Thomas Fuller
(English Churchman & Historian)
富勒（英国牧师、史学家）

哀莫大于心死。

——战国·宋·庄子（思想家、哲学家、文学家）
《庄子·田子方》
Zhuangzi (Philosopher & Writer)

A wise man never loses anything if he has himself.

——Friedrich Wilhelm Nietzsche
(German Philosopher)
尼采（德国哲学家）

只要生命存在，失去的永远不是全部。

——郭延庆
《失去的与拥有的》
Guo Yanqing

74

留得青山在，不怕没柴烧。

——明·凌蒙初（小说家）
《初刻拍案惊奇》卷二十二
Ling Mengchu (Novelist)

It is defeat that turns bone to flint; it is defeat that turns gristle to muscle; it is defeat that makes men invincible. Do not then be afraid of defeat. You are never so near to victory as when defeated in a good cause.

——Henry Ward Beecher
(American Clergyman, Social Reformer)
比彻（美国神职人员、社会改革者）

失败乃成功之母。

——谚语
Chinese Proverb

Homer sometimes nods.

——Proverb
西方谚语

神仙也有打盹的时候。

——俗语
Chinese Proverb

人有失手，马有失蹄

——俗语
Chinese Proverb

Too many cook spoil the broth.

——Proverb
西方谚语

鸡多不下蛋，人多大瞎乱。

——俗语
Chinese Proverb

A fall into the pit, a gain in your wit.

——Proverb
西方谚语

吃一堑，长一智。

——明·王阳明
（思想家、哲学家、军事家）
《与薛尚谦书》
Wang Yangming
(Philosopher & Militarist)

None are so blind as those who won't see.

——Proverb
西方谚语

充耳不闻。

——《诗经·邶风·旄丘》
Chinese Proverb

视而不见。

——《礼记·大学》
Chinese Proverb

chapter 10

> Strike the shepherd, and the sheep will be scattered.

——*Jesus*
(Founder of Christianity)
耶稣(基督教创始人)

> 树倒猢狲散。

——北宋·庞元英(进士)
《谈薮·曹咏妻》
Pang Yuanying (Scholar)

> Truth sits upon the lips of dying men.

——Matthew Arnold
(British Poet & Critic)
马修•阿诺德(英国诗人、评论家

> 心有余而力不足。

——春秋·孔子(思想家、教育家)
《论语·里仁》
Confucius (Philosopher & Educator)

Human Nature 人性

No one can make you feel inferior without your consent.

——Franklin D. Roosevelt
(32nd President of the United States)
罗斯福(美国第三十二任总统)

没有人在世界上能够"弃"你，除非
你自己自暴自弃，因为我们是属于
自己的，并不属于他人。

——三毛(作家)
San Mao (Author)

The spirit indeed is willing but the flesh is weak.

—— *Jesus*
(Founder of Christianity)
耶稣(基督教创始人)

78

人之将死，其言也善；鸟之将死，
其鸣也哀。

——春秋·孔子(思想家、教育家)
《论语·泰伯》
Confucius (Philosopher & Educator)

Mediocrity knows nothing higher than itself, but talent instantly recognizes genius.

——Arthur Conan Doyle
(Scottish Writer)
柯南·道尔（苏格兰作家）

燕雀安知鸿鹄之志哉。

——西汉·司马迁（史学家、文学家、思想家）
《史记·陈涉世家》
Sima Qian (Historian, Writer & Philosopher)

The pot calls the kettle black.

——Miguel de Cervantes
(Spanish Novelist & Poet)
塞万提斯（西班牙小说家、诗人

彼此彼此。

——清·郭小亭（小说家）
《济公全传》
Guo Xiaoting (Novelist)

五十步笑百步。

——战国·孟子（思想家、哲学家）
《孟子·梁惠王上》
Mengzi (Philosopher)

Human Nature　人性

——F.H. Bradley
(British Idealist Philosopher)
布拉德利(英国唯心主义哲学家)

There are persons who, when they cease to shock us, cease to interest us.

语不惊人死不休。

——唐·杜甫(现实主义诗人)
Du Fu (Poet)

Your own property is concerned when your neighbor's house is on fire.

——Horace
(Ancient Roman Lyric Poet)
贺拉斯(古罗马抒情诗人)

邻家失火，不救自危。

——谚语
Chinese Proverb

80

城门失火，殃及池鱼。

——北齐·杜弼(军事家)
《檄梁文》
Du Bi (Militarist)

古今中外隽语妙对

There is something about the outside of a horse that is good for the inside of a man.

——Winston Churchill
(British Former Prime Minister & Statesman)
丘吉尔（英国前首相、政治家）

龙马精神。

——唐·李郢（进士）
Li Ying (Scholar)

——明·冯梦龙（文学家）
《醒世恒言》第三十五卷
Feng Menglong (Writer)

江山易改，禀性难移。

Can a leopard change its spots?

——Bible
《圣经》

Change of scene is not change of nature.

——Aesop
(Greek Fable Writer)
伊索（希腊寓言作家）

Human Nature　人性

A long dispute means that both parties are wrong.

——Voltaire
(French Philosopher, Historian & Writer)
伏尔泰（法国哲学家、史学家、作家）

孤掌难鸣。

——战国·韩非子
（哲学家、政论家、散文家）
《韩非子·功名》
Han Feizi
(Philosopher, Political Commentator & Essayist)

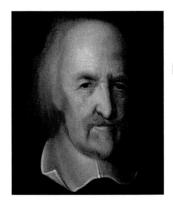

Give him an inch he'll take an ell.

——Thomas Hobbes
(English Philosopher)
托马斯·霍布斯（英国哲学家）

得寸进尺。

——春秋·西周·老子（哲学家、思想家）
《道德经》
Laozi (Philosopher)

> **Suspicion always haunts the guilty mind; the thief doth fear each bush an officer.**
>
> ——William Shakespeare
> (English Dramatist)
> 莎士比亚（英国剧作家）

> **君子坦荡荡，小人长戚戚。**
>
> ——春秋·孔子（思想家、教育家）
> 《论语》
> Confucius (Philosopher & Educator)

> **Man's greatness lies in his power of thought**
>
> ——Blaise Pascal
> (French Philosopher Mathematician)
> 帕斯卡（法国哲学家、数学家）

> **人们的社会存在，决定人们的思想。而代表先进阶级的正确思想，一旦被群众掌握，就会变成改造社会、改造世界的物质力量。**
>
> ——毛泽东
> （革命家、中国共产党、新中国领导人）
> Mao Zedong (Revolutionist & Communist)

Human Nature 人性

By ignorance is pride increased; Those who assume most who know the least.

——John Gay
(English Poet)
约翰·盖伊（英国诗人）

一知半解的人，多不谦虚；
见多识广有本领的人，一定谦虚。

——谢觉哉（学者、教育家）
Xie Juezai (Scholar & Educator)

忽视所短，可以自满。

——茅以升（桥梁学家、教育家）
Mao Yisheng (Engineer & Educator)

84

越是没有本领的人，
就越加自命不凡。

——邓拓（政论家）
Deng Tuo (Political Commentator)

You and I are not what we eat;
we are what we think.

——Walter Anderson (Businessman)
沃尔特·安德森（商人）

兵贵神速，人贵思索。

——春秋·孙子（军事家）
《孙子·九地》
Sunzi (Militarist)

Too much cleverness is folly.

——Solon
(Ancient Athenian Statesman, Lawmaker & Lyric Poet)
梭伦（古代雅典政治家、立法者、抒情诗人）

机关算尽太聪明，反算了卿卿性命。

——清·曹雪芹（小说家）
《红楼梦》
Cao Xueqin (Novelist)

Human Nature 人性

The greatest genius often lies concealed.

——Johann Wolfgang von Goethe
(German Novelist & Poet)
歌德（德国小说家、诗人）

真人不露相。

——明·吴承恩（小说家）
《西游记》
Wu Cheng'en (Novelist)

卧虎藏龙。

——北周·庾信（作家）
《同会河阳公新造山地聊得寓目》
Yu Xin (Author)

Where do you hide a leaf? In the middle of the forest. Where do you hide a dead body? In a field of massacre.

——G.K. Chesterton
(British Journalist & Novelist)
切斯特顿（英国记者、小说家）

大隐隐于市。

——唐·白居易（诗人）
《中隐》
Bai Juyi (Poet)

大智若愚。

——北宋·苏轼（词人、书画家）
《贺欧阳少师致仕启》
Su Shi (Poet & Painter-calligrapher)

古今中外隽语妙对

He only may criticize who loves.

——William Shakespeare
(English Dramatist)
莎士比亚（英国剧作家）

你没有接近过它，你便没有权利轻视。

——张抗抗（作家）
《埃菲尔铁塔沉思》
Zhang Kangkang (Auhtor)

The mind is it's own place, and in itself, can make a heaven of hell, and a hell of heaven.

——John Milton
(British Poet)
约翰·弥尔顿（英国诗人）

天堂不是一个现实的去处，只是心灵的一个去处，天堂存不存在并不重要，重要的是心中有没有天堂。

——徐国静（诗人、演说家）
Xu Guozheng (Poet & Lecturer)

Human Nature 人性

A goodly apple rotten at the heart. O, what a goodly outside falsehood hath!

——William Shakespeare
(English Dramatist)
莎士比亚（英国剧作家）

刘基

金玉其外，败絮其中。

——明・刘基（军事家、诗人）
《卖柑者言》
Liu Ji (Militarist & Poet)

空有其表。

——唐・郑处诲（进士）
《明皇杂录》
Zheng Chuhai (Scholar)

90

表里不一。

——《逸周书・谥法解》
Chinese Proverb

古今中外隽语妙对

There are three types of baseball players—those who make it happen, those who watch it happen, and those who wonder what happened.

——Tommy Lasorda
(American Pitcher)
汤米·拉索达（美国投手）

人有三种，先知先觉，
后知后觉，不知不觉。

——孙中山（近代中国的民主革命家）
Sun Zhongshan (Revolutionist)

Queer thing how trouble acts different on folks: it's like hot weather—sours milk but sweetens apples.

——Joseph Crosby Lincoln
(American Novelist)
约瑟夫·克罗斯比·林肯

火，只能把铁炼成钢，却无法把
铁烧为灰烬。

——刘白羽（散文家、小说家）
Liu Baiyu (Essayist & Novelist)

Human Nature 人性

After the event, even a fool is wise.

——Homer
(Greek Epic Poet)
荷马（希腊史诗诗人）

放马后炮。

——清·夏敬渠（小说家）
《野叟曝言》第29回
Xia Jingqu (Novelist)

有缺点的战士终究是战士，
完美的苍蝇也终究不过是苍蝇。

——鲁迅（文学家、思想家、革命家）
Lu Xun (Writer, Philosopher & Revolutionist)

You know you can put lipstick on a
pig, but it's still a pig.

——Barack Obama
(44th President of the United States)
奥巴马（美国第四十四任总统）

If a jewel falls into the mire,
it remains as precious as before;
and though dust should ascend to
heaven, its former worthlessness
will not be altered.

——Jaber
贾比尔

古今中外隽语妙对

> **Superiority has always been detested, and most thoroughly when greatest**

——Baltasar Gracian
(Spanish Prose Writer)
巴尔塔沙·葛拉西安（西班牙散文作家）

> 志士幽人莫怨嗟，
> 古来材大难为用。

——唐·杜甫（现实主义诗人）
《古柏行》
Du Fu (Poet)

> 新官上任三把火。

——俗语
Chinese Proverb

> A new broom sweeps clean.

——Proverb
西方谚语

> Who hoalds a power but newly gained is ever stern of mood.

——Aeschylus
(Ancient Greek Playwright)
埃斯库罗斯（古希腊剧作家）

Human Nature　人性

Do not engage with him who has nothing to lose, because unaccounted even to shame; and having auctioned off everything, he has nothing to lose.

——Baltasar Gracian
(Spanish Prose Writer)
巴尔塔沙·葛拉西安（西班牙散文作家）

哀兵必胜。

——春秋·西周·老子（哲学家、思想家）
《老子》第六十九章
Laozi (Philosopher)

穷寇莫追。

——春秋·孙子（军事家）
《孙子·军争》
Sunzi (Militarist)

94

狗急跳墙。

——《敦煌变文集·燕子赋》
Chinese Proverb

He knows, who knows that
he does not know.

——Baltasar Gracian
(Spanish Prose Writer)
巴尔塔沙·葛拉西安（西班牙散文作家）

有不知则有知，无不知则无知。

——北宋·张载（哲学家）
《张载集》
Zhang Zai (Philosopher)

Poverty sits by the cradle of all our
great men and rocks all of them to
manhood.

——Heinrich Heine
(German Romantic Poet)
海涅（德国浪漫诗人）

成德每在困穷。

——清·王豫（画家）
《蕉窗日记》
Wang Yu (Painter)

Human Nature　人性

Applause is the spur of noble minds, the end and aim of weak ones.

——Charles Caleb Colton
(English Writer & Collector)
科尔顿（英国作家、收藏家）

败身多因得志。

——清·王豫（画家）
《蕉窗日记》
Wang Yu (Painter)

A liar begins with making falsehood appear like truth and ends with making truth itself appear like falsehood.

——William Shenstone
(English Poet)

威廉　申斯通　（英国诗人）

真作假时假亦真。

——清·曹雪芹（小说家）
《红楼梦》
Cao Xueqin (Novelist)

96

He shines in the second rank, who is eclipsed in the first.

——Voltaire
(French Philosopher, Historian & Writer)
伏尔泰（法国哲学家、史学家、作家）

宁为鸡口，无为牛后。

——《战国策·韩策一》
Chinese Proverb

The chain of friendship, however bright, does not stand the attrition of constant close contact.

——Sir Walter Scott
(Scottish Historical Novelist & Poet)
沃尔特·斯科特爵士（苏格兰历史小说家、诗人）

相见易得好，久住难为人。

——《增广贤文》
Chinese Proverb

Friends are lost by calling often and calling seldom.

——Scottish Proverb
苏格兰谚语

Human Nature 人性

The heart is a small thing, but desireth great matters.
It is not sufficient for a kite's dinner, yet the whole world
is not sufficient for it.

——Victor Marie Hugo
(French Playwright & Novelist)
雨果（法国剧作家、小说家）

人心不足蛇吞象。

——《山海经·海内南经》
Chinese Proverb

The infinitely little have a pride infinitely great.

——Voltaire
(French Philosopher, Historian & Writer)
伏尔泰（法国哲学家、史学家、作家）

欲壑难填。

——《国语·晋语八》
Chinese Proverb

There are three wants which can never be satisfied: that
of the rich who wan something more; that of the sick,
who want something different; and that of the traveler,
who says, "anywhere but here."

——Ralph Waldo Emerson
(American Philosopher & Writer)
爱默生（美国哲学家、文学家）

A tree is known by its fruit.

——Jesus
(Founder of Christianity)
耶稣（基督教创始人）

观其行而知其人。

——谚语
Chinese Proverb

Be careful of the person who does not talk, and the dog that does not bark.

——Proverb
西方谚语

明枪易躲，暗箭难防。

——《独角牛》
Chinese Proverb

无声狗咬死人。

——俗语
Chinese Proverb

知人知面不知心。

——元·尚仲贤（戏曲作家）
《单鞭夺槊》第二折
Shang Zhongxian (Dramatist)

Human Nature　人性

Among the blind the one-eyed man is king.

——Proverb
西方谚语

山中无老虎，猴子称霸王。

——俗语
Chinese Proverb

池里无鱼虾自大。

——俗语
Chinese Proverb

After death, the doctor.

——Proverb
西方谚语

事后孔明。

——俗语
Chinese Proverb

Fair without, false within.

——Proverb
西方谚语

在家凶如狮，在外怯如鼠。

——谚语
Chinese Proverb

Everybody's business is nobody's business.

——Daniel Defoe
(English Writer & Journalist)
笛福（英国作家、记者）

两人养马瘦，两人养船漏。

——俗语
Chinese Proverb

一个和尚挑水喝，两个和尚抬水喝，三个和尚没水喝。

——谚语
Chinese Proverb

Men can acquire knowledge but not wisdom. Some of the greatest fools ever known were learned men.

——Spanish Proverb
西班牙谚语

笨人做不了最笨的事，最笨的事都是聪明人做的。

——李敖（学者、作家、评论家）
Li Ao (Scholar, Author & Critic)

Its not stupid sons that ruin the family.

——Anonymous
佚名

Human Nature 人性

The heart is deceitful above all things.

——Bible
《圣经》

人们总以为自己最理解自己，其实我们最容易不知不觉地被自己所蒙骗。

——盛晓明（作家）
Sheng Xiaoming (Author)

Behold, I send you forth as sheep in the midst of wolves: be ye therefore wise as serpents, and harmless as doves.

——Bible
《圣经》

害人之心不可有，防人之心不可无。

——明·洪应明
《菜根谭》
Hong Yingming (Author)

A man may lead a horse to the water, but he cannot make him drink.

——Thomas Heywood
(English Dramatist)
托马斯·海伍德（英国剧作家）

牛不饮水怎按得牛头低。

——谚语
Chinese Proverb

The true genius shudders at incompleteness- and usually prefers silence to saying something which is not everything it should be.

——Edgar Allan Poe
(American Poet)
爱伦·坡（美国诗人、短片小说作家）

明哲保身。

——《诗·大雅·烝民》
Chinese Proverb

不求有功，但求无过。

——俗语
Chinese Proverb

Never swap horses while crossing the stream.

——Abraham Lincoln
(16th President of the United States)
林肯（美国第十六任总统）

临阵换将，兵法大忌。

——成语
Chinese Proverb

骑渡中流莫换马，病重不宜换郎中。

——俗语
Chinese Proverb

Human Nature　人性

Even evil men know how to give good gifts to their children.

——Bible
《圣经》

虎毒不食子。

——南宋·释普济(医家、僧人)
《五灯会元·杭州龙华寺灵照真觉禅师》
Shi Puji (Doctor & Monk)

虎毒不吃儿。

——明·吴承恩(小说家)
《西游记》
Wu Cheng'en (Novelist)

The grass is always greener on the other side.

——Proverb
西方谚语

自家的肉不香,人家的菜有味。

——俗语
Chinese Proverb

外来的和尚好念经。

——俗语
Chinese Proverb

Human Nature 人性

Chapter 11

——北宋·释道原（作家）
《景德传灯录·卷十·
赵州东院从稔禅师》
Shi Daoyuan (Author)

抛砖引玉。

Modesty is the only sure bait when you angle for praise

——Philip Stanhope
(British Statesman)
菲利普·斯坦霍普
（英国政治家，文学家）

天不言而四时行，
地不语而百物生。

——唐·李白（浪漫主义诗人）
Li Bai (Poet)

Ants are more diligent than any other animal, and notice how they always keep silent.

——Benjamin Franklin
(American Statesman & Scientist)
富兰克林（美国政治家、科学家）

Silence is the element in which great things fashion themselves.

——Thomas Carlyle
(British Essayist & Historian)
托马斯·卡莱尔（苏格兰散文家、历史学家）

＼ Talking 言论

三人成虎。

——战国·韩非子
（哲学家、政论家、散文家）
《韩非子·内储说上》
Han Feizi
(Philosopher, Political Commentator & Essayist)

Make the lie big make it simple, keep saying it, and eventually they will believe it.

——Adolf Hitler
(Head of State of the Nazi Party)
希特勒（德国纳粹党领袖）

病从口入，祸从口出。

——西晋·傅玄（政治家、文学家、思想家）
《口铭》
Fu Xuan (Politician, Writer & Philosopher)

What defines a man is not what goes into his mouth, but what proceeds from it.

——Jesus
(Founder of Christianity)
耶稣（基督教创始人）

A man may dig his grave with his teeth.

——Proverb
西方谚语

贼喊捉贼。

——南朝·宋·刘义庆(文学家)
《世说新语·假谲》
Liu Yiqing (Writer)

He that first cries thief is often the thief himself.

——William Congreve
(English Playwright)
威廉·康格里夫(英国剧作家)

一个不去尊重别人的人不配受人尊重;一个没有爱人之心的人也同样无权享受别人的爱。

——盛晓明(作家)
Sheng Xiaoming (Author)

Honor begets honor; trust begets trust; faith begets faith; and hope is the mainspring of life.

——Henry Lewis Stimson
(American Statesman)
亨利·刘易斯·史汀生(美国政治家)

Talking　言论

一言既出，驷马难追。

——春秋·孔子（思想家、教育家）
《论语·颜渊》
Confucius (Philosopher & Educator)

The tongue is a beast, which once at large, is hard to recapture and to chain.

——Baltasar Gracian
(Spanish Prose Writer)
巴尔塔沙·葛拉西安（西班牙散文作家）

——北宋·释道原（作家）
《景德传灯录》卷六
Shi Daoyuan (Author)

君子一言，快马一鞭。

108

Once a word has been allowed to escape, it cannot be recalled.

——Horace
(Ancient Roman Philosopher)
贺拉斯（古罗马抒情诗人）

至言不繁。

——北宋·苏轼（词人、书画家）
Su Shi (Poet & Painter-calligrapher)

Brevity is the soul of wit.

——William Shakespeare
(English Dramatist)
莎士比亚（英国剧作家）

—— Proverb
西方諺語

Actions speak louder than words.

事实胜于雄辩。

——鲁迅（文学家、思想家、革命家）
《<热风>题记》
Lu Xun (Writer, Philosopher & Revolutionist)

Talking　言论

Talking　言论

All is but lip-wisdom that wants experience.

——Philip Sidney
(British Statesman)
菲利普·西德尼（英国政治家）

纸上谈兵。

——西汉·司马迁（史学家、文学家、思想家）
《史记·廉颇蔺相如列传》
Sima Qian (Historian, Writer & Philosopher)

闭门造车。

——南宋·朱熹（思想家、哲学家）
《中庸或问》卷三
Zhu Xi (Philosopher)

纸上得来终觉浅，
绝知此事要躬行。

——南宋·陆游（诗人）
《冬夜读书示子聿》
Lu You (Poet)

The proof of the pudding is in the eating.

——Proverb
西方谚语

For evil news rides fast, while good news baits later.

——John Milton
(British Poet)
约翰·弥尔顿（英国诗人）

好事不出门，坏事传千里。

——俗语
Chinese Proverb

Bees that have honey in their mouths have stings in their tails.

——Scottish Proverb
苏格兰谚语

口蜜腹剑。

——北宋·司马光（政治家、文学家、史学家）
《资治通鉴》
Sima Guang (Politician, Writer & Historian)

佛口蛇心。

——南宋·释普济（医家、僧人）
《五灯会元》卷二十
Shi Puji (Doctor & Monk)

＼ Talking　言论

Do not live what you preach, but preach what you live.

——Proverb
西方谚语

君子耻其言而过其行。

——春秋·孔子（思想家、教育家）
《论语》
Confucius (Philosopher & Educator)

He who can lick can also bite.

——English Proverb
英国谚语

成也萧何，败也萧何。

——南宋·洪迈（文学家）
《容斋续笔·萧何给韩信》
Hong Mai (Writer)

水能载舟，亦能覆舟。

——战国·赵·荀子（思想家、政治家）
《荀子·哀公篇》
Xunzi (Philosopher & Politician)

好面誉人者，亦好背而毁之。

——战国·宋·庄子（思想家、哲学家、文学家）
《庄子·盗跖》
Zhuangzi (Philosopher & Writer)

The same breast feeds both criminals and saints alike.

——Anonymous
佚名

水是一样，牛喝了便成乳汁，蛇喝了便成毒液。

——许地山（作家、学者）
《缀网劳蛛》
Xu Dishan (Author & Scholar)

It is better to remain silent and be thought a fool than to open your mouth and remove all doubt.

——Samuel Johnson
(British Essayist & Poet)
塞缪尔·约翰逊（英国散文家、诗人）

Let a fool hold his tongue and he will pass for a sage.

——Publilius Syrus
(Assyrian Latin Writer of Maxims)
希如斯（叙利亚-拉丁格言作家）

你不说话没人当你是傻瓜。

——俗语
Chinese Proverb

Talking　言论

A bad workman always blames his tools.

——Proverb
西方谚语

自恨枝无叶，莫怨太阳偏。

——谚语
Chinese Proverb

The man who can't dance thinks the band is no good.

——Polish Proverb
波兰谚语

不会睡觉怪床歪。

——俗语
Chinese Proverb

A man of words and not of deeds is like a garden full of weeds.

——Proverb
西方谚语

少说空言，多做实事。

——巴金(小说家)
Ba Jin (Novelist)

A bad workman always blames his tools.

——Proverb
西方谚语

自恨枝无叶，莫怨太阳偏。

——谚语
Chinese Proverb

The man who can't dance thinks the band is no good.

——Polish Proverb
波兰谚语

不会睡觉怪床歪。

——俗语
Chinese Proverb

A bird is known by its note, and a man by his talk.

——Proverb
西方谚语

闻弦歌而知雅意。

——《吕氏春秋》
Lu Buwei (Businessman,
Politician & Philoopher)

Talking 言论

A picture shows me at a glance what it takes dozens of pages of a book to expound.

——Ivan Turgenev
(Russian Novelist)
伊凡·屠格涅夫
（俄国小说作家）

一画胜千言

——谚语
Chinese Proverb

Still water runs deep.

——Proverb
西方谚语

半瓶醋，乱晃荡。

——俗语
Chinese Proverb

非宁静无以致远。

116

——三国·蜀·诸葛亮
（政治家、外交家、发明家、
军事理论家）
《诫子书》
Zhuge Liang (Politician, Inventor,
Military Theorist)

Chapter 12

强行者有志。

——春秋·西周·老子(哲学家、思想家)
《老子》第三十三章
Laozi (Philosopher)

Be studious in your profession, and you will be learned. Be industrious and frugal and you will be rich. Be sober and temperate, and you will be healthy. Be in general virtuous, and you will be happy.

——Benjamin Franklin
(American Statesman & Scientist)
富兰克林(美国政治家、科学家)

Every noble work is at first impossible.

——Thomas Carlyle
(British Essayist & Historian)
托马斯·卡莱尔(苏格兰散文家、历史学家)

万事起头难。

——清·黄小配(小说家)
《大马扁》第七回
Huang Xiaopei (Novelist)

On Diligence　勤奋

勤能补拙。

——北宋·邵雍（哲学家）
《弄笔吟》
Shao Yong (Philosopher)

When I was young I observed that nine out of every ten things I did were failures, so I did ten times more work.

——George Bernard Shaw
(Irish Playwright)
萧伯纳（爱尔兰剧作家）

If you have great talents, industry will improve them; if you have but moderate abilities; industry will supply their deficiency

——Joshua Reynolds
(English Painter)
雷诺（英国画家）

勤能补拙是良训，
一分辛劳一分才。

——华罗庚（数学家、作家）
Hua Luogeng (Mathmatician & Author)

118

笨鸟先飞早入林。

——俗语
Chinese Proverb

"不耻最后"。即使慢，驰而不息，纵令落后，纵令失败，但一定可以达到他所向的目标。

——鲁迅（文学家、思想家、革命家）
Lu Xun (Writer, Philosopher & Revolutionist)

I walk slowly, but I never walk backwards.

——Abraham Lincoln
(16th President of the United States)
林肯（美国第十六任总统）

By perseverance the snail reached the ark.

——Charles H. Spurgeon
(England Prince of Preachers)
查尔斯·哈登·司布真（英国基督教传教士）

不怕慢就怕站。

——俗语
Chinese Proverb

On Diligence 勤奋

On Diligence　勤奋

Even though you are on the right track you will get run over if you just sit there.

——Will Rogers
(American Comedian)
威尔·罗杰斯（美国喜剧演员）

天下事不兴则亡，不进则退，
不自立则自杀。

——邹容（革命演说家）
《革命军》
Zou Rong (Revolutionary Speaker)

不是前进，便是被人踩死。

——茅盾（文学家）
Mao Dun (Writer)

任何人，不管他的天资如何好，成就
多么大，只要停止了努力就不能继续
进步。今天不努力，明天就落伍。

——钱伟长（数学家、教育家）
Qian Weichang (Mathmatician & Educator)

古今中外隽语妙对

七分人事三分天。三分天资，人人得而有之，七分人事，人人能之而未必得。

——张大千（画家）
Zhang Daqian (Painter)

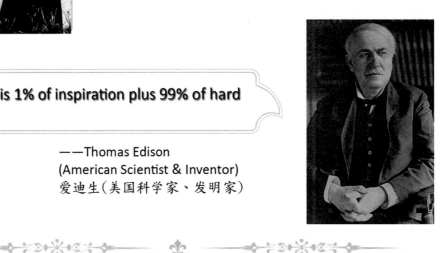

Genius is 1% of inspiration plus 99% of hard work.

——Thomas Edison
(American Scientist & Inventor)
爱迪生（美国科学家、发明家）

古之立大事者，不惟有超世之才，亦必有坚忍不拔之志。

——北宋·苏轼（词人、书画家）
《晁错论》
Su Shi (Poet & Painter-calligrapher)

The right road to distinction is that of merit, and when industry is joined to worth, it is a short cut to the stars.

——Baltasar Gracian
(Spanish Prose Writer)
巴尔塔沙·葛拉西安（西班牙散文作家）

On Diligence　勤奋

天与不取，反受其咎；时至不行，反受其殃。

——西汉·司马迁（史学家、文学家、思想家）
《史记·越王勾践世家》
Sima Qian (Historian, Writer & Philosopher)

He who will not when he may, when he will, shall have nay.

——Proverb
西方谚语

I succeeded because I willed it, I never hesitated.

——Napoleon Bonaparte
(French Military & Political Leader)
拿破仑（法国军事、政治领导人）

当断不断，反受其乱。

——西汉·司马迁（史学家、文学家、思想家）
《史记·齐悼惠王世空》
Sima Qian (Historian, Writer & Philosopher)

当机立断。

——东汉·陈琳（文学家）
《东阿王笺》
Chen Lin (Writer)

122

——南宋·陈元靓（作家）
《事林广记》第九卷
Chen Yuanliang (Author)

世上无难事，只怕有心人。

A strong passion for any object will ensure success, for the desire of the end will point out the means.

——William Hazlitt
(British Essayist)
威廉·赫兹利特（英国散文家）

三思而后行。子闻之曰：
"再，斯可矣。"

——春秋·孔子（思想家、教育家）
《论语·公冶长》
Confucius (Philosopher & Educator)

To think too long about doing a thing often becomes its undoing.

——Eva Young
(First Lady of Argentina from 1946 to1952)
伊娃·杨（1946年-1952年间阿根廷第一夫人）

We don't have enough time to premeditate all our actions.

——Vauvenargues
(French Moralist & Essayist)
沃夫纳格（法国道德家、散文家）

\ On Diligence   勤奋

The early bird catches the worm.

——Proverb
西方谚语

捷足先登。

——西汉·司马迁（史学家、文学家、思想家）
《史记·淮阴侯列传》
Sima Qian (Historian, Writer & Philosopher)

Chapter 13

读书不必求多，而要求精。

——邓拓（政论家）
Deng Tuo (Political Commentator)

A small number of choice books are sufficient.

——Voltaire
(French Philosopher, Historian & Writer)
伏尔泰（法国哲学家、史学家、作家）

读书贵精熟　不要贪多。

——明·胡居仁（理学家）
Hu Juren

In the case of good books, the point is not to
see how may of them you can get through, but
rather how many can get through to you.

——Mortimer Adler
(American Philosopher)
莫迪默·艾德勒（美国哲学家）

On learning　向学

学而不思则罔，
思而不学则殆。

——春秋·孔子（思想家、教育家）
《论语·为政》
Confucius (Philosopher & Educator)

To read without reflecting is like eating
without digesting.

——Edmund Burke
(Irish Political Theorist)
埃德蒙·伯克（爱尔兰政治理论家）

有学而无问，虽读书万卷，
只是一条钝汉尔。

——清·郑板桥（书画家）
Zheng Banqiao (Painter-calligrapher)

A man may as well expect to grow stronger by
always eating as wiser by always reading.

——Jeremy Collier
(English Theologian)
杰里·科利尔（英国神学家）

126

He who nothing questions, nothing learns.

——Stephen Gosson
(French Philosopher)
笛卡尔（法国哲学家）

三人行，必有我师焉。

——春秋·孔子（思想家、教育家）
《论语·述而》
Confucius (Philosopher & Educator)

I am defeated, and know it, if I meet any human being from whom I find myself unable to learn anything.

——George Herbert Palmer
(American Scholar & Author)
乔治·赫伯特·帕尔默（美国学者、作家）

莫等闲，白了少年头，空悲切。

——岳飞（民族英雄、军事家、抗金名将）
《满江红》
Yue Fei (Militarist)

Who so neglects learning in his youth, loses the past and is dead for the future.

—— Euripides
(Ancient Greek Tragic Dramatist)
欧里庇德斯（古希腊悲剧剧作家）

Stand firm, look back, be resolute, and beware. Why did not honest Work thy Youth employ? Contemplate, Mortal, on thy fleeting Years.

——John Gay
(English Poet)
约翰·盖伊（英国诗人）

On learning 向学

学问之成立在于信，
而学问之进步则在疑。

——蔡元培（教育家）
《蔡元培教育文选》
Cai Yuanpei (Educator)

The beginning of wisdom is found in doubting.
By doubting we come to the question, and by
seeking we may come upon the truth.

——Pierre Abelard
(French Medieval Scholastic Philosopher)
皮埃尔　阿伯拉德
（法国中世纪经院哲学家）

不能为已成的学说压倒，
不怀疑不能见真理。

——李四光（科学家、地质学家、教育家）
Li Siguang (Scientist, Geologist & Educator)

128

If you would be a real seeker after truth, it is
necessary that at least once in your life you
doubt, as far as possible, all things.

——Rene Descartes
(French Philosopher)
笛卡尔（法国哲学家）

知之必好之，好之必求之，
求之必得之。

—— 北宋·程颢（教育家）
《河南程氏遗书》
Cheng Hao (Educator)

No profit is taken where there is no joy, In
short sir, study what thou most affect.

——William Shakespeare
(English Dramatist)
莎士比亚（英国剧作家）

书籍是贮存人类代代相传的智慧
的宝库。

——季羡林（古文字学家、翻译家、史学家）
Ji Xianlin (Philologist, Translator & Historian)

Who will limit the price of the infinite treasure
of books, from which the scribe who is instructed
bringeth forth things new and old?

——Richard De Bury
(English Writer)
理查德·德·伯利（英国作家）

On learning　向学

On learning　向学

夫人好学，虽死若存；不学者，
虽存，谓之行尸走肉耳。

——东晋·王嘉(炼丹人)
《拾遗记·后汉》卷六
Wang Jia (Alchemist)

Many peoples tombstones should read "died at 30, buried at 60".

——Nicholas Murray Butler
(American Philosopher, Diplomat & Educator)
尼古拉斯·默里·巴特勒(美国哲学家、外交官、教育家)

All men fear to die, but what they should fear is to have never lived.

——William Wallace (Scottish Knight)
Brave Heart Movie
威廉·华莱士(苏格兰骑士)

刘向

书犹药也，善读之可以医愚。

——西汉·刘向(文学家)
Liu Xiang (Writer)

There are more men ennobled by study than by nature.

——Marcus Tullius Cicero
(Ancient Roman Orator, Politician & Philosopher)
西塞罗(古罗马政治家、哲学家)

Man is born the barbarian, and only culture redeems him from the bestial.

——Baltasar Gracian
(Spanish Prose Writer)
巴尔塔沙·葛拉西安(西班牙散文作家)

人不学，不知义。

——《三字经》
Chinese Proverb

If you believe everything you read, you better not read.

——English Proverb
英国谚语

尽信书不如无书。

——战国·孟子(思想家、哲学家)
《孟子·尽心下》
Mengzi (Philosopher)

The difference between the right word and the almost right word is the difference between lightning and the lightning bug.

——Mark Twain
(American Novelist)
马克·吐温(美国小说家)

The difference between Playoff and Layoff excites such contrary emotions that one can hardly imagine that the difference is but two alphabets.

——Amy Lee
(Chinese Teacher)
李邱湄(中文教师)

差之毫厘，谬以千里。

——《礼记·经解》

On learning 向学

It is not shame for a man to learn that which he knows not, whatever his age.

——Socrates
(Ancient Greek Philosopher)
苏格拉底（古希腊哲学家）

白首穷经。

——《元史·张特立传》
Chinese Proverb

The tombstone will be my diploma.

——Eartha Kitt
(American Actress)
鄂莎·基特（美国演员）

活到老，学到老。

——俗语
Chinese Proverb

The education of a man is never completed until he dies.

——Robert Edward Lee
(American General)
罗伯特·爱德华·李（美国将军）

The world is a book, and those who do not travel read only a page.

——Proverb
西方谚语

读万卷书，行万里路。

——明·董其昌（书画家）
《画旨》
Dong Qichang (Painter-calligrapher)

听君一席话，胜读十年书。

——《增广贤文》
Chinese Proverb

I would never read a book if it were possible for me to talk half an hour with the man who wrote it.

——Woodrow Wilson
(28th President of the United States)
威尔逊（美国第二十八任总统）

It is with narrow-minded people as with narrow necked bottle; the less they have in them the more noise they make in pouring out.

——Alexander Pope
(English Poet)
亚历山大·蒲柏（英国诗人）

水深不响，水响不深。

——谚语
Chinese Proverb

小人自大，小溪声大。

——俗语
Chinese Proverb

洪钟无声，满瓶不响。

——小儿语
Chinese Proverb

On learning 向学

The force of union conquers all.

——Homer
(Greek Epic Poet)
荷马（古希腊诗人）

三个臭皮匠，胜过一个诸葛亮。

——谚语
Chinese Proverb

A cord of three stands is not easily broken.

——Bible
《圣经》

分则小，小则弱；合则大，大则强。

——清·康有为（社会改革家、书法家、学者）
《共和政体论》
Kang Youwei
(Revolutionist, Scholar)

Many hands make light work.

——Proverb
西方谚语

众人拾柴火焰高。

——俗语
Chinese Proverb

134

And how can man die better than facing fearful odds, For the ashes of his fathers And the temples of his gods?

——Thomas Babington Macaulay
(British Poet & Historian)
托马斯·巴宾顿·麦考利（英国诗人、史学家）

为国捐躯，虽死犹荣。

——俗语
Chinese Proverb

——清·徐骧（爱国将领）
Xu Xiang (General)

大丈夫为国捐躯，死而无憾。

And for our country 'tis a bliss to die.'

——Homer
(Greek Epic Poet)
荷马（希腊史诗诗人）

Who would not be that youth? What pity is it that we can die but once to save our country!

——Joseph Addison
(English Essayist & Poet)
约瑟夫·阿狄森（英国散文家、诗人）

Society/ Politics   社会与政治

民为贵，社稷次之，君为轻。

——战国·孟子(思想家、哲学家)
《孟子·尽心下》
Mengzi (Philosopher)

The people are the masters of their own country.

——Edmund Burke
(Irish Statesman)
埃德蒙·伯克(爱尔兰政治理论家)

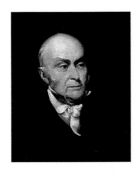

The die was now cast; I had passed the Rubicon. Swim or sink, live or die, survive or perish with my country was my unalterable determination.

——John Quincy Adams
(6th President of the United States)
约翰·昆西·亚当斯(美国第六任总统)

捐躯赴国难，视死忽如归。

——三国·魏·曹植(诗人)
《白马篇》
Cao Zhi (Poet)

投死为国，　以义灭身。

——三国·魏·曹操(军事家、政治家、诗人)
Cao Cao (Militarist, Politician & Poet)

136

If you do good? Who are they that persecute you? Silence others by doing good.

——St. Paul
(Apostle of Jesus)
圣保罗（耶稣的使徒）

政者，正也。子帅以正，
孰敢不正？

——春秋·孔子（思想家、教育家）
《论语·颜渊》
Confucius (Philosopher & Educator)

All mankind my brether, the world is my home, and to do well my religion.

——William Blake
(English Poet & Painter)
威廉·布莱克（英国诗人、画家）

居天下之广居，立天下之正位，
行天下之大道···此之谓大丈夫

——战国·孟子（思想家、哲学家）
《孟子·滕文公下》
Mengzi (Philosopher)

四海之内，皆兄弟也。

——春秋·孔子（思想家、教育家）
《论语·颜渊》
Confucius (Philosopher & Educator)

Society/ Politics　　社会与政治

Mothers all want their sons to grow up to be president, but they don't want them to become politicians in the process.

——John F. Kennedy
(35th President of the United States)
约翰·F. 肯尼迪（美国第三十五任总统）

但愿生儿愚且鲁，无灾无难到公卿。

——北宋·苏轼（词人、书画家）
Su Shi (Poet & Painter-calligrapher)

无知是愚昧的温床。

——柯灵（编辑）
Ke Ling (Editor)

Better be unborn than untaught, for ignorance is the root of misfortune.

——Plato
(Ancient Greek Philosopher)
柏拉图（古希腊哲学家）

138

If you think education is expensive try ignorance.

——Derek Curtis Bok
(American Educator & Lawyer)
德里克·柯蒂斯·博克
（美国教育家、律师）

> For forms of government let fools contest; whatever is best administered is best.

——Alexander Pope
(English Poet)
亚历山大·蒲柏（英国诗人）

> 不管黑猫白猫，
> 捉到老鼠就是好猫。

——邓小平（政治家、军事家、外交家）
Deng Xiaoping (Politician, Militarist & Diplomat)

> All who have meditated on the art of governing mankind have been convinced that the fate of empires depends on the education of youth.

——Aristotle
(Ancient Greece Philosopher)
亚里士多德（古希腊哲学家）

> 要有良好的社会， 必先有良好的个人，要有良好的个人， 必先有良好的教育。

——蔡元培（教育家）
《蔡元培教育文选》
Cai Yuanpei (Educator)

> 教育为立国根本。

——陶行知（教育家）
Tao Xingzhi (Educator)

Society/ Politics　　社会与政治

一时强弱在于力，
千秋胜负在于理。

——曹禺（戏剧家）
Cao Yu (Dramatist)

A man may build himself a throne of bayonets,
but he cannot sit on it.

——William Ralph Inge
(English Author)
威廉·拉尔夫·英格（美国作家）

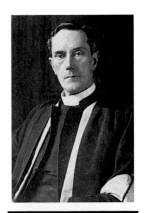

Force is all conquering, but its victories are
short lived.

——Abraham Lincoln
(16th President of the United States)
林肯（美国第十六任总统）

140

It is not strength, but art, obtains the prize,
And to be swift is less than to be wise. Tis
more by art, than force of numerous strokes.

——Homer
(Greek Epic Poet)
荷马（希腊史诗诗人）

王子犯法与庶民同罪。

——西汉·司马迁（史学家、文学家、思想家）
《史记·商君列传》
Sima Qian (Historian, Writer & Philosopher)

No man is above the law and no man is below
it; nor do we ask any man's permission when we
require him to obey it. Obedience to the law is
demanded as a right; not asked as a favor.

——Theodore Roosevelt
(26th President of the United States)
西奥多·罗斯福（美国第二十六任总统）

政之所兴，在顺民心。
政之所废，在逆民心。

——春秋·管仲（政治家、军事家）
《管子·牧民》
Guan Zhong (Politician & Militarist)

The will of the people is the only legitimate
foundation of any government, and to protect
its free expression should be our first object.

——Thomas Jefferson
(3rd President of the United States)
杰斐逊（美国第三任总统）

Society/ Politics 社会与政治

There is no unity without you and I.

——Proverb
西方谚语

独木不成林。

——汉·崔骃（学者）
《达旨》
Cui Yin (Scholar)

Stuck between a rock and a hard place.

——Proverb
西方谚语

进退维谷。

——《诗经》
Chinese Proverb

Those who foolishly sought power by riding the back of the tiger ended up inside.

——John F. Kennedy
(35th President of the United States)
约翰·F.肯尼迪（美国第三十五任总统）

民惟邦本，本固邦宁。

——《尚书·五子之歌》
Chinese Proverb

Dictators ride to and fro upon tigers which they dare not dismount. And the tigers are getting hungry.

——Winston Churchill
(British Former Prime Minister & Statesman)
丘吉尔（英国前首相、政治家）

骑虎难下。

——《明史·袁化中传》
Chinese Proverb

Government of the people, by the people, for the people.

——Abraham Lincoln
(16th President of the United States)
林肯（美国第十六任总统）

Acknowledgement　鸣谢

　　经过两年多繁重而艰辛的选编工作后，这本书终于完成了。我们很幸运，得到迪奕网络科技(上海)有限公司的鼎力支持和帮忙。在编写的过程中，因为我们的精益求精，从封面、封底的设计、人物肖像的挑选、中英文的字形、内页的构图到书中选录的佳句，我们都一改再改，修改了无数次。牵一发而动全身。但迪奕网络科技(上海)有限公司完全能配合我们的要求，给我们提供了专业的、细致的、高效率的服务，使这本书今天能呈献给亲爱的读者们·为此，我们衷心地向迪奕网络科技(上海)有限公司致以最真诚的感谢！
同时，要谢谢该公司负责美工的臧迪生先生，他的专业知识、他的美术眼光，使这本书看上去雍容、优雅；更要谢谢该公司负责校对和翻译的沈慧小姐，她细心、耐心、中英文知识渊博，使这本书得以近乎完美·

李邱湄
臧迪凯

　　First and foremost, this book could not have been completed in two years time without Dream Express's editorial and design team. Their professionalism could only be matched with the passion they have shown towards every detail of this work. We would like to thank Cherry for her editorial work and Edison for his design of Confucius Meets Shakespeare, and both of them for their pursuit for clarity, design, and correctness —a phenomenal work.
We never could have finished compiling this book, though, without the continuous support of our family and friends; I believe Saint Augustine said it best, "faith is to believe what you cannot see and the reward of faith is to see what you believed," and we want to thank you for having faith in us.

Amy Lee
Joseph Tsang